Re-Imagining Evangelization

✱ *Patrick J. Brennan*

Re-Imagining Evangelization

✱ *Toward the Reign of God and the Communal Parish*

CROSSROAD · NEW YORK

1995
The Crossroad Publishing Company
370 Lexington Avenue, New York, NY 10017

Library of Congress Cataloging-in-Publication Data

Brennan, Patrick J.
    Re-imagining evangelization : toward the reign of God and the
communal parish / Patrick J. Brennan.
        p.   cm.
    ISBN 0-8245-1433-5
    1. Evangelistic work.   2. Pastoral theology—Catholic Church.
3. Kingdom of God.   4. Catholic Church—Membership.   I. Title.
BX2347.4.B74   1994
266'.001—dc20
                                                        94-29500
                                                        CIP

To Helen Canty Brennan . . .
who first gave me life,
love, and faith . . .

Contents

Preface 1

1 · Jesus and the Reign of God 5

2 · Conversion: Goal of Pastoral Ministry 31

3 · Toward Original Wholeness and Communion 39

4 · Enabling the Empowered 45

5 · Toward the Communal Parish 50

6 · The Communal Parish 70

7 · Ministry to Conversion Readiness 98

8 · The Nominal Christian: Concerns and
Strategies 105

9 · Ministry in the Communal Parish 124

10 · Pastoral Planning as Planning
for Evangelization 135

11 · The Magnet Parish, the Marketing Plan 146

12 · Generation "X" and Midlifers 155

Epilogue 165

Bibliography 167

Preface

*F*or the last fifteen years, I have dedicated myself to serving as an advocate for Catholic evangelization. The advocacy has been for the broad, rich vision articulated in Paul VI's *Evangelii nuntiandi*, as well as for innovative strategies that help with this, the Church's essential mission. I have often said, in lectures as well as in written material, that the best strategies are grown locally and organically, by parishes or clusters of parishes in alliance.

In writing this book, I find myself in a new place: with a real concern for the essence of our evangelical mission—what Jesus meant by the Reign of God. All evangelization is toward that reality. We need to spend much more time trying to discern what Jesus meant by that metaphor. We need also to better understand the multilayered dynamics of conversion, for conversion is the necessary prerequisite for life in God's Reign.

It seems to me that the constitutive element of the vision and practice of God's Reign is communion, or community. In fact I sense contemporary people hungering and thirsting for three realities: meaning, healing, and connection. The congregations and parishes that help people in these three heart searches will be the effective evangelizing organisms of the future. This book places great emphasis on the question of developing community. I believe if community begins to be experienced, the other two elements of acquiring meaning and experiencing intra- and interpersonal healing will follow.

In an age of diminishing resources and dwindling numbers of priests, I give special emphasis to the priesthood of the faithful. In making such an advocacy, I do not intend to present the ministry of the baptized as a second-class, temporary reaction until historically we move into a new era of quantitative and qualitative improvement in the area of a male, celibate clergy. The clergy shortage and the explosion of baptismal ministries are parallel occurrences. But I perceive baptismal ministries as indeed the will of God and a movement of the Holy Spirit. In this book, I present ministerial training of the baptized as a profoundly spiritual work, unleashing the gifts of the Spirit in a congregation.

As we move toward a new millennium, we populate both a church and a world changing at ever-increasing rates. The rapidity of change creates an anxiety that often is ameliorated by people of differing ideologies retreating into fundamentalism that is idiosyncratic to a particular worldview and ecclesiology. There are liberal fundamentalists and conservative fundamentalists in the church today. With their politicizing and power moves, they threaten the life of the church they claim to love. The new millennium and young people around the globe need us to become a generative church, in dialogue and collaboration with one another as we seek to hand on the best of "the tradition" to those younger than we. I hope this book, which is a synthesis of theologizing and pastoral practice, contributes to the needed ongoing conversation.

Again my profound thanks to Michael Leach of Crossroad Publications for the opportunity to write again and for his patience about several missed deadlines. Thanks also to

Dawn Mayer Melendez who was both patient and long-suffering in dealing with the manuscript as it slowly evolved on paper and on tape.

I have come to value imagining and re-imagining as the conception moments in the birthing of new movements and processes for evangelization. I hope the book is experienced and used not as an end in itself but as a catalyst in the reader's imagination— re-imagination—or birthing process. As new pastoral models emerge, we are sharing in the work of God, the work of creation.

Patrick Brennan
April 25, 1994

Jesus and the Reign of God

A colleague and I recently did an afternoon of reflection with future Master of Divinity students. Our subject was the future of the church. During one of the group processing sessions, we solicited the students' feelings about the church that is to come. A variety of responses came forth—-from fear and a feeling of paralysis to genuine enthusiasm. One student was especially focused. He said that for all appearances a number of factors affecting Roman Catholics would suggest that we are "in the worst of times": declining numbers of clergy, diminishing numbers attending worship, financial difficulties, and scandals largely involving clergy. On the other hand, he suggested that these apparent crisis years could paradoxically be the best of times. With the decline of outmoded structures and encouragement toward more innovative models of ministry, and with the *laos theou,* the People of God, creatively assuming responsibility for their church, this death moment in the church could possibly be a genuine rebirth.

A bishop spoke in a similar vein to me recently in a private conversation that we had. He said, "I really believe God is

rendering this church poor. I believe God is bringing us to
our knees—especially those of us who are leaders in the
church. We have been doing it "our way," and our way is not
God's way. The recent experience of the Catholic Church
resembles the experience of people in Twelve Step processes. We are losing and will lose a lot. But in all this loss
and dying, perhaps we are being led to a more genuine, real
encounter with God. And maybe God is refashioning the
church the way God wants it."

Both the students and the bishop, certainly at two ends
of the continuum when it comes to church, reaffirmed in
me a core conviction. The church is not an end unto itself.
The church is a servant to a reality greater than itself—
God's Kingdom, God's Reign. In *Evangelii nuntiandi* (1975)
Paul VI impressed upon the church the centrality of God's
Reign in the ministry of Jesus. In Mark 1:15, Jesus says, "I
have good news for you . . . The Reign of God is near. . . .
change your lives." The same precise simplicity can be found
in Matthew 4:19 and Luke 4:43. Perhaps many of us in the
evangelization movement have too much, too often stressed
structural renewal in our talks and writings. Structural renewal is certainly important. But structural renewal can only
flow from a retrieval of the vision that such structures are
supposed to facilitate. We too often have jumped to strategies
without spending sufficient time on the mission.

As pastoral workers and ministers we need to be about
what Jesus was about. Jesus' mission revolved around the
Reign of God. It is important that we try to understand more
than we have in the past what that image meant to Jesus.
Understanding God's Reign is no easy task. Not one of the
evangelists presents Jesus giving a clear definition or de-
scription of God's Reign. God's Reign is encased in the
preaching, teaching, healing, and ministry of Jesus. We

must deduce from parables, narrative accounts, and miracles what God's Reign means.

God's Reign is an alternative dimension to life, or an alternative to the mundane, status quo, obsessive-compulsive, nonreflective culture that we move through daily. In no way can we build the Kingdom of God. God's Kingdom, God's Reign *is*. To put it another way, God reigns! God is the sovereign, the cosmic authority of all creation and life. We can pay attention to God's Reign, cooperate with God's Reign, facilitate more and more the emergence of God's Reign, help each other pay attention to the inbreaking of God in each of our lives—but we cannot build it.

Donald Senior, C.P., and Carroll Stuhlmueller, C.P., in their important book, *The Biblical Foundations of Mission*, make a good attempt at describing what Jesus intended by God's Reign. Life in the Reign of God involves replicating the radical spirituality of Jesus, his Abba-centeredness, his unique piety in our lives. Life in God's Reign involves continuing the work of Jesus, especially in his ministry of reconciliation, forgiveness, healing, and liberation or exorcism. Kingdom living involves the consciousness that all of creation can become one, especially the human family. God's dream is communion and connectedness, theologian-philosopher Richard Westly says. The God of Jesus' preaching is an expansive God, larger than any image mainline churches have created. Membership in God's family is expansive and inclusive, not narrow like the elitist, hierarchical parameters often set by churches. God's Reign consists of all humanity in an egalitarian communion with the Creator, the Higher Power, the cosmic and unconditionally loving parent at the center.

In his parables and teachings and healings, Jesus suggests that God's Reign includes what follows. The Reign of God refers to God's subtle but real presence in all of life. God is involved in our story, in human history. God wills salvation for all, and that salvation is participated in through one's grounding in God. Life in God's Reign is a life that recognizes God's sovereignty. God alone can claim allegiance in a cosmic sea of spiritualities and meaning systems. People of the Kingdom pursue God's will and plan; they realize their ultimate powerlessness and God's great power. God's love in this Kingdom is universal, intended for all of creation. Thomas Groome suggests that the constitutive elements of God's Reign contain the satisfaction of the human heart's deepest hungers and thirsts for meaning, belonging, love, and freedom. Jesus began to understand himself as the definitive revelation and unfolding of God's Reign. In the eleventh chapter of Matthew's Gospel, when asked by John's disciples whether he (Jesus) is "the one to come . . . or do we look for another?," Jesus replies, "Go back and report to John what you hear and see: the blind recover their sight, cripples walk, lepers are cured, the deaf hear, the dead are raised to life, and the poor have the good news preached to them." Thus, Jesus seems to describe what he understands to be Kingdom activities, and himself as the incarnation of them.

> The Kingdom/God's Reign is obviously visionary in nature. By that I mean it is a way of life, an outlook on life. Life in God's Reign is the foundational experience of one's self as an unconditionally loved son or daughter of God. God's Reign changes self-concepts. Changed self-concepts in turn change one's outlook on others. If all are equally loved by God, we are then brothers and sisters to one another. Centering one's life on God's centrality and sovereignty moves a person toward the discarding of all false security and illusions. The meaning of life is found in the quality of one's love and service. The God of the Kingdom

is near to us, not remote as sometimes espoused by organized religion.

Other words characterize those who dwell in God's Kingdom: freedom, discernment, and vigilance in many different
areas of life; prayerfulness, trust, surrender, nonaggression,
a core conviction that life is paschal in nature, always from
life through death to new life. Life in God's Reign is countercultural, always rubbing against the status quo of both organized religions and the dominant culture.

God's Reign consists of people in the process of redemption cooperating with God in the redemption of the world.
Kingdom people are impelled by a sense of mission and a
covenant of responsibility toward the world. They are breaking out of spiritual lukewarmness and privatized religion.
People of the Kingdom are engaged always in the process of
moral conversion and behavioral faith; they are people who
make peace and *work* for justice.

And though the Reign of God is here (realized eschatology), it simultaneously is not yet, is always in process, is
still seeking fulfillment. As one returning missionary student
once said to me in class: "Admitting the truth of all the
previous theologizing, God's Reign must be incarnated—a
people, in a place, in time, in community— trying to continue the mission of Jesus."

The mission of Jesus was to announce and to demonstrate
God's Reign. That mission now has a church as its deacon,
as its servant. We always need to keep in mind the instrumentality of the church. At this writing it seems important
to state again what many might think to be obvious or simplistic. I believe it is important to restate it in this period
that Gerald Arbuckle has called a time of restorationism.
Arbuckle believes that current Roman Catholic leadership,
rather than using the turn of the century as a time to "re-
found" the church around evangelization and innovative pas-

toral strategies, is instead attempting to "restore" the church to pre-Vatican II theology and praxis. It is an extremely important time to restate Vatican II's ideal that the church is in fact the People of God. All of the baptized are, then, part of the instrumentality of the church. All have responsibility and accountability for the Kingdom. All of us are gifted by the Holy Spirit. None of us can sit back and allow church professionals to "do church" for us. As recent Call to Action conferences in Chicago have proclaimed: "We are the Church!" But CTA also poses a question after that statement: "What would the church be like if we acted on that? How much more would the mission of God's Reign be advanced if more us acted as if we are the church?"

Grounded in Scripture

Any integral re-imagining of evangelization needs a firm grounding in Scripture. As we have already stated, the ministry of evangelization is intimately connected with experience—God's Reign as experienced by Jesus. Evangelization seeks to invite people to an experience similar to that of Jesus. Thus, efforts in the last twenty years to evangelize by getting bodies into or back into pews are anemic at best. They miss the point of evangelization. To evangelize we must try as best we can to recapture the mind, the inner world of Jesus relative to God's Reign. Though many ancient writings exist to help us in this quest, the best and most frequently relied on are the four Gospels and the Epistles of St. Paul. I would add that if we are to grow in the skills of apologetics, or being able to articulate our faith, we should add to our foundational documents the fathers and mothers of Christian antiquity, the decisions of the great Christological councils, and ancient credal formulas. We begin with the oldest canonical Gospel, that of Mark.

Mark: Discipleship and the Cross

Though a version of Matthew in Aramaic seems to have pre-dated Mark, his is the oldest canonical Gospel, written around A.D. 64. Mark is said to have been a colleague of Peter and also a companion of Paul. He is writing for a church undergoing persecution and martyrdom. The lens through which Mark presents God's Reign, therefore, is the cross, the mystery of suffering. Jesus is the Messiah, the embodiment of God's Reign. If the price he had to pay for the mission was suffering and death, so must it be for his followers.

As mentioned earlier, the first words of Jesus in Mark's Gospel are an announcement of God's Reign as imminent and present, and a call to conversion or repentance to better be a part of God's Reign.

Of significance is a statement by Jesus in Mark 3:34, 35. When informed that his mother, brothers, and sisters are outside looking for him, Jesus responds, "Here are my mother and brothers. Anyone who does the will of God, that person is my brother and my sister and my mother." Jesus is making a revolutionary statement here. No longer are blood ties or family of origin the undergirding relationships in one's life. There is another bond that unites men and women in another family, God's family, synonymous with God's Reign. The bond that connects us is placing God at the center of life, seeking his will in life, first over all other matters.

A further expansion on Jesus' acceptance of the Father's will, and in fact the turning point of Mark's Gospel, can be found in Mark 8:27–38. Jesus asks his disciples who people think that he, Jesus, is. They give various replies. Peter is reported as giving a very pointed reply. He says that he believes Jesus is the Christ, the anointed one who is to come into the world for the salvation of God's people. Jesus concurs with Peter's answer, but then goes on to speak of a growing intuition that he is having. This Christ, this Messiah will be rejected by the leaders of institutionalized religion, be persecuted by them and ultimately put to death. But death will not be the victor. The Son of Man (a title we will look at momentarily) will rise three days after his death. Peter cannot tolerate such talk about this concept of a Messiah or Christ. As he tries to correct Jesus' vision of things, Jesus reprimands him by referring to him as *Satan,* and accusing him of judging by human standards rather than according to God's will. It seems to be God's will that Jesus experience the ordeal ahead of him. And he struggled to accept that divine will and plan as part of the unfolding of the Kingdom. Jesus goes on to say that the cost of discipleship, of following him, will always be the cross, in the myriad ways it has come into believers' lives over the last two thousand years.

The Markan emphasis on the title Son of Man has roots in the Old Testament Book of Daniel, chapter 7 and following. The Son of Man is an otherworldly being of power and majesty who chose lowliness to serve the needs of others. Besides the Son of Man, there is another formulation that Mark is known for: the Messianic secret. In chapter nine's account of the transfiguration, and elsewhere after performing miraculous cures, Jesus admonishes his followers not to tell anyone about the out-of-the-ordinary events. Often, however, the recipients of his healing touch spread the word anyway. For Mark, the nature of Jesus' messianic role is an unfolding secret, emerging from the cryptic self-description, Son of Man. The secret is not clarified until chapter 15 when Jesus dies. The pagan centurion standing by exclaims, "In truth, this man was the Son of God." Jesus was God's own Son, crucified by the forces of sin and evil present in people and systems. The tearing of the temple veil in Mark apparently signifies the end, the ineffectiveness of the Old Law.

In Mark, as in other Gospel accounts, there is both the call of apostles and the commissioning of them for the work of the Kingdom. Of great importance is that the ministry of the Kingdom is connected with healing. The twelve are given authority over unclean spirits. This Markan detail points toward what we should be doing in evangelization in our own day—namely, bringing God's good news to people as we try to minister to their needs and wounds and share with them the healing power of God at work through us. I often think of the late Mark Searle's words, when several of us asked him in the late 1980s how he would suggest we could improve evangelization efforts in the Catholic Church. His response took us by surprise. Searle said that the church ought to take steps to restore its devotional life. Mass on Sunday, while the summit of our faith, is not enough. People need the richness of eucharistic food supplemented by other prayer experiences. Searle went on to say such a restored devotional life needs to be focused on reality and on healing. His words came back to me as I participated in a healing service for a friend and pastoral musician, Mary Ellen Leibewein, who was dying of cancer several years ago. Several hundred of us gathered in the parish church to pray over, talk with, and lay hands on Mary Ellen. It was one of the most powerful experiences I have ever had in a church. All who were there felt ministered to and evangelized by the experience together. Since that Friday night, I have often wondered if parishes ought not to do similar things on a regular basis for others, with the ill, the dying, the out of work, the addicted, and on and on. Such reality-based prayer experiences would have greater "existential" impact than many of our typical program efforts.

Finally, Mark presents a Jesus who became silent before Pilate. "Greatly to Pilate's surprise, Jesus made no further response" (Mark 15:5). Jesus' silence seems to speak of a radical reliance on one power alone at this point— the love and providential care of Abba.

Matthew: Jesus, the Teacher of a New Way

It is clear among Scripture scholars that the author of the Gospel attributed to Matthew was not the tax collector called by Jesus in the Gospels. There are several theories as to how this Gospel developed. Some contend that a school of Jewish scribes who converted to Christianity produced a handbook of Christian conduct for teachers. Another theory, called "The Two Source" theory, says that Matthew is essentially an editing together of Mark with sayings of Jesus that have come to be known as "Q." The multisource theory says that a more ancient text, Matthew in Aramaic, plus another version of Matthew in Greek, plus materials possibly from Peter, plus Mark and "Q" have given us the current Matthew.

Jesus as teacher is the central motif of Matthew. He is presented as the new teacher, up against the spiritually bankrupt teachers, the scribes and Pharisees. Matthew was written in a Jewish environment, probably around A.D. 85. It seems to have been written for those who had converted to Christianity from Judaism. There is in the Gospel a profound Jewishness, but the Gospel simultaneously suggests the author and his community have split with their roots in Judaism. Thus, for Matthew, Jesus is the fulfillment of what was hoped for by the Jews. Matthew, in fact, organizes his material in five main sections, or books, suggesting an arrangement like the Pentateuch, the first five books of the Jewish Bible. Even in literary construction, Matthew is making a statement: the Pentateuch, or Old Law, came from Moses; but in this Gospel we have the New Law, from the new Moses, Jesus. Matthew's Gospel traces Jesus' genealogy or roots back to Abraham, again emphasizing Jesus' Jewishness and Jesus as the fulfillment of the Old Law. The slaughter of innocents and the flight into Egypt are reminiscent of events surrounding the birth of Moses in Exodus, chapter 1, and again suggest a Moses-Jesus parallel.

Chapter 4 of Matthew depicts the call of Peter, Andrew, James, and John. One must note the immediacy of their responsiveness to Jesus and their willingness to let go of attachments to follow him. Matthew positions Jesus on a hill delivering the evangelical discourse. The new Moses reveals the new order of reality. God and God's Kingdom are breaking through in unexpected people and places: in the lowly, the gentle, the peacemakers—in effect, wherever false security has been abandoned and people have come to realize their total reliance on God's power, grace, and love. In this sermon on the mount, extending over chapters 5, 6, and 7 of Matthew, Jesus calls his followers to make a difference in society, to be salt and light for the world. He challenges them and us to transcend the typical expectations of organized religion, and to live lives of purified attitudes and values. Charity is to be done out of love for strangers. In prayer, God is to be imaged and addressed as a loving Parent. In prayer, we should praise God, pray for the advancement of God's Reign and the unfolding of his will. We should address God concerning our perceived needs. We should seek both God's forgiveness and the strength to forgive others. We should be conscious of the forces of evil around us and seek God's grace in resisting evil.

Chapter 11 of Matthew gives us further insight into the mind of Jesus regarding God's Reign. John the Baptist, in prison, sends representatives to Jesus to ask if he is the one to come or whether John and his followers should look for another. Jesus says to go back to John with the message: the blind are seeing, the lame are walking, lepers are cleansed, the deaf are hearing, the dead are rising to life, and the poor are hearing Good News. Such is the nature of God's Reign. It is the experience of people, in their broken humanity, discovering healing and meaning through divine presence and ministerial mediation.

Parables in all the Gospels fall into three categories. Some of Jesus' parables are "advent" parables. These speak of how God and God's Reign enter our history. Others are "reversal" parables. They change typical expectations about how God is. Others are "action" parables. They basically communicate that once a person finds God and God's Kingdom, some behavior change or action is needed. In speaking of God's Reign as a mustard seed and yeast in bread, Jesus is speaking through two advent parables. He is speaking of God's presence in life as subtle, yet real and influential. There is no mustard tree without the seed. There is not bread without yeast. Speaking of the Kingdom as buried treasure and a valuable pearl, Jesus is speaking through action parables. When a person finds the buried treasure or the pearl, he or she goes and sells everything to buy the valuable new discovery. God's Reign demands that we get rid of some things so that we can "buy into" God's will and plan.

The nature miracle of Jesus walking on the water is a lesson on the power of faith. Through reliance on divine power, we have strength and abilities that transcend our own imaginings. In chapter 16, the theology of Matthew intimately connects the Kingdom of God with the church. The church is an incarnation of God's Kingdom, and Peter holds a special role in the church. Peter is given the power to bind and loose, which was an old rabbinic privilege to judge the moral propriety or impropriety of synagogue members— in effect to discern whether they were worthy of belonging. In chapter 18, some of the style of that church is described by Jesus. Kingdom-church members are servants. They have an enthusiasm for God's Reign that resembles the enthusiasm of a child. They are conscious of the power of both good and bad example to others, especially to the young. They, like God, are concerned not just about collectives, but the individual, and realize the importance of seeking out even one person who is lost or in need. People of the Kingdom-church engage in existential, real-life reconciliation when there is conflict or disagreement among members. They are forgiving of past injuries. It is the experience of Jesus' followers that, when they gather together to pray, Jesus is present among them.

The parable of the vineyard laborer in Matthew 20 and of the wedding feast in Matthew 22 are powerful statements about the expansive nature of the Kingdom of God. It is inclusive of all, if people respond to God's invitation. There is no divine exclusivity or elitism in God's Reign. These parables resemble those in Luke, like the Prodigal Son, or the Good Samaritan, in "reversing" our expectations of God. They are called "reserval parables." Also in Matthew 22, the preeminence of love and compassion as the commandments for someone consciously living in God's Reign is articulated. This is reinforced in chapter 25, where Jesus describes the last judgment and says that we will be judged in light of our mercy, love, and compassion.

The anguish of Jesus in the garden in Matthew 26 is the context for yet another articulation of a core value of God's

Reign. In great distress, Jesus is still able to articulate "Your will be done." Jesus' admonition of Peter for cutting off the high priest's ear in 26:52–53 is a clear statement regarding the nonaggression that characterizes life in God's Reign. In chapter 27 we witness again the silence of Jesus, revealing that inner solidarity Jesus had with Abba. The tearing of the temple veil, also in chapter 27, symbolizes the end of the Old Law and the beginning of a new order.

The resurrection of Jesus in Matthew's Gospel explodes into mission. Matthew 28:16–20 has been adopted by many evangelical churches or movements as their foundational charter. In fact the passage is referred to by many as "the great commissioning." Jesus sends the community gathered by his resurrection to the world: "Go . . . to the world . . . make disciples . . . teach them all the commands that I gave you."

Luke: The Universal Jesus

Luke traveled with and was influenced by Paul. Unlike Matthew, whose approach was decidedly Jewish, Luke writes instead for the Gentile world. The Jesus of Luke reaches out to and is open to all types of people: minority groups, segregated groups, the underprivileged, shepherds, the poor, Samaritans, lepers, politicians, public sinners, and others. Luke's Gospel is connected with issues of social justice. The God that Jesus reveals is a God of mercy, compassion, and forgiveness. This just and merciful God is found in the parable of the Prodigal Son, the story of Zacchaeus, and the repentant thief on the cross. The poor are often depicted as the recipients of God's special choice or selection. Women are presented in a very positive light in Luke's Gospel—a very countercultural image for the time. Whereas

Matthew's genealogy traced Jesus' Jewish roots, Luke traces Jesus to Adam—an implicit statement that Jesus is meant for the entire human family. The evangelical discourse in Luke is delivered on a plain—Jesus speaking on level ground for all types of people. This is a contrast to Matthew's Mosaic-like sermon on the mount.

Luke places special emphasis on the power of prayer. The power and role of the Holy Spirit is likewise emphasized, culminating in the coming of the Holy Spirit in the second chapter of the Acts of the Apostles. Acts is a kind of volume two of Luke.

Tradition has it that Luke's background was that of a physician. Perhaps that is why in Luke we notice a sensitivity to psychological detail. In both 9:51 and 19:28 Luke speaks of Jesus' resolve to move toward Jerusalem, despite what awaited him there. Luke portrays a stark loneliness about Jesus during his last days: he taught at the temple during the day, then spent nights on the Mount of Olives. He would return to the temple early in the morning. The resolve to move toward Jerusalem, and his ability to continue to minister despite his lonely burden, reveal a strong bond between Jesus and the Father. That strong bond is even more revealed in the last words of Jesus as he dies. He quotes Psalm 31 in saying: "Father, into Your hands I commend my Spirit." Donald Senior speaks of Jesus' "Abba spirituality" or piety, which was at the heart of Jesus' experience of the Kingdom of God.

The commissioning of the disciples does not come at the end of Luke's Gospel, as it does in Mark and Matthew. The disciples' mission will not begin until a later time when they will be "clothed with power from on high." The coming of the Spirit happens in Luke volume two, or the second chapter of that second volume, the Acts of the Apostles. As Acts unfolds, the ministry and mission of the church parallels that of Jesus.

The Johannine Jesus

Two main blocks of material can be found in John's Gospel. The Book of Signs extends from 1:19 to 12:50. In the Old Testament, the Israelites always met God in and through powerful signs that God worked in their midst. John chose the word *sign* over miracles in his Gospel. The meaning is similar to the Old Testament mindset. God was experienced through the signs worked through Jesus. The second block of material in John is called the Book of Exaltation, extending from 13:1 to 20:31. In this section, Jesus instructs his disciples in a long farewell discourse (13:1–17:26). We witness the glorification of Christ in chapters 18:1 through 20:31. In John, the Resurrection appearance and the giving of the Holy Spirit are experienced as seamless, united events.

Raymond Brown, through careful research of John's Gospel, teaches that the Gospel arose from a community that started around someone known as "the beloved disciple." The disciple knew Jesus during his ministry. It is dated somewhere around A.D. 90.

Relative to the other three Gospels, John's Gospel is more theological. There is a great deal of implicit ecclesiology (theology of church) and sacramentology (theology of sacraments). There is realized eschatology in John, meaning John's Jesus speaks of people actually experiencing God's judgment in the present based on the style and quality of their lives. John's Christology teaches that Jesus is the incarnate word of God, who in turn gives us a share in divinity.

John's Gospel is highly stylized, intended for a Hellenistic audience. He is also heavily into symbolism. The calling of the apostles takes place in seven days, symbolizing a kind of "new creation." The signs that Jesus worked are precisely seven in number: the miracle at Cana, the cure of the nobleman's son at the seventh hour, the cure at the pool of Bethsaida, the miracle of the loaves, the walking on water, the cure of the blind man, and the raising of Lazarus.

Several chapters reveal John's ecclesiology, sacramentology, and symbolism quite clearly. When Jesus speaks to the woman at the well in chapter 4, the author strategically places her at Jacob's well, which symbolizes the Old Law. Jesus tells the woman that water from that old well will never satisfy her thirst, but that Jesus can give her water that springs up as a fountain within. The symbolism and baptismal imagery are apparent.

John is the only evangelist who does not include an institutional narrative for the Eucharist. Yet his rich eucharistic theology can be found in chapter 6. A very important evangelical insight into the sacramental life is contained in chapter 6. In 6:35, Jesus speaks of himself as the Bread of Life, that whoever comes to him in a personal relationship will never be hungry. In 6:51, he again speaks of himself as the Bread of Life. In this reference, he says that whoever eats the Bread will live forever. There is great importance in the sequence of the two Bread of Life references. Essentially what Jesus is saying is that one ought to come to him in a personal relationship before ritualizing by eating the Eucharist. Conversion and sacramentalizing need always to be integrated. In the ninth chapter, in the curing of the blind man, Jesus anoints the man's eyes with a paste made of saliva and dirt. The paste seems to symbolize the anointing at Baptism. The implicit theology is that Baptism gives one new sight or new vision.

Some important Johannine themes follow:

- the darkness of the world and Jesus as light;
- Jesus as the Word of God;
- the love of God for all of creation;
- love as the essence of discipleship;
- the signs;
- the glory of God reflected in Jesus before his death, more fully revealed in the Resurrection, now present in us and in the ministry of the church;
- the return of Jesus to the Father (the preexistence of Christ before his earthly life);
- faith as a way of knowing and seeing;
- faith that leads to love;
- the sending of the Spirit; the Spirit as the life force of Jesus' divine sonship;
- eternal life (or condemnation) as already begun;
- the church and sacraments as extensions of Christ's glorification and life in the Spirit to us.

The Christ Jesus of Paul

Someone who has greatly contributed to the Jesus we relate to today is Paul. Saul (Paul) was a Pharisaical Jew and a Roman citizen from Tarsus. He seems to have been well educated, middle class, with both Hebrew and Roman values, certainly influenced by both the Pharisaical and Gentile worlds. The encounter that he had with Jesus on the road to Damascus caused him to reinterpret his life totally. He became gifted with extraordinary insight into God's plan and the significance of Jesus.

Recurring Pauline themes are:

- in Jesus, God has entered human history and begun a New Age;
- the human and divine now interpenetrate because of Christ;
- the solidarity of all people in Christ;
- personal faith;
- death and resurrection; the cross;
- agape, or the love we are all called to;
- election, or God's choice of us and grace;
- the work of the Spirit;
- redemption and justification.

Paul continued the early Christology of the church, preaching and writing about the "crucified and risen one" in the years between the oral transmission of the kerygma and the writing of the Gospels.

His letters follow a standard outline:

(1) an opening formula

(2) thanksgiving for the community to which he is writing

(3) the message

(4) a conclusion and final greeting.

The main body of Paul's work can be divided into three categories: his anthropology, largely found in Galatians; his soteriology, largely found in Romans and Philippians; his teaching on community life, largely found in I and II Corinthians.

Relative to anthropology, Paul saw all of humanity in a corporate state before Christ. All were sinners, under the power of sin. Connected to sin is the power of death; because we are sinners, we must die. The Old Testament law, which at one point in history was useful, now actually multiplies sin. Without Christ, human beings could not achieve the purpose for which they were created.

Paul's soteriology, or understanding of Jesus as the Savior, sees Jesus as a salvific force let loose in the world with cosmic, universal implications. God had a plan that has unfolded in four stages:

(1) the period before Moses;

(2) the period from Moses to Christ;

(3) the actual experience of Christ;

(4) us, the church.

The mission of Christ was a positive, evolutionary step in the unfolding of the Father's plan. Christ is the center of all life and creation. Jesus is the revelation of the Father, his plan, and the way human beings should be. The Father's plan involves the salvation of the human family. The life, death, and Resurrection of Jesus are decisive moments in the plan. In Paul's theory of salvation Christ has:

(1) paid the price for the sin of Adam (expiation, satisfaction);

(2) redeemed the human race, bringing us back from estrangement and alienation;

(3) reconciled us with the Father;

(4) justified us; juridically speaking, made us "OK" in the eyes of God.

Paul has a rather undefined pneumatology, or theology of the Spirit. The Spirit is:

(1) the mode or way of experiencing Jesus;

(2) the gift of God's presence;

(3) God's power.

In calling Jesus *Kyrios* or Lord, Paul has raised him to a status equivalent to Yahweh. The Father made Jesus *Kyrios*, or Lord, at the Resurrection. For Paul the historical Jesus became the glorified Christ who conquered sin, suffering, and death, and who shares that victory with us. Through Baptism we share in both his death and his resurrection.

Post-Scriptural Christological Development

Besides Sacred Scripture, other forces have contributed to our understanding of Jesus and His mission. The Nicene Creed (325 A.D.) and the Apostles' Creed (sixth century) rather clearly state the central tenets of our convictions about Jesus Christ. The Didache (100–150 A.D.) contain the beginnings of liturgical formulations in the early Christian community as well as legislation for communal living. The Fathers of the Church greatly added to the tradition about Jesus. While we cannot cover all of them in any great depth, several are included here to round out this journey:

(1) Ignatius of Antioch, an apostolic father, that is, in line with the tradition of the apostles: strongly defended the unity of the humanity and divinity of Jesus;

(2) St. Justin, a Greek father, further developed the notion of Jesus as *logos*, or Word of the Father;

(3) St. Irenaeus of Lyons developed the Pauline notion of Jesus as a step in the Father's plan. He spoke of Jesus as the second Adam, the *homo futurus*—the person we all need to become like. His evolutionary view of Jesus is known as *recapitulation* and became foundational to the thought of Teilhard de Chardin;

(4) Tertullian, an African, taught that Jesus is one person but both God and man. He speaks of the cross as the price Christ paid for our sins.

In addition to the Fathers, much Christology came to us from Church Councils responding to heresies.

(1) **The Council of Nicea** (325 A.D.) defined consubstantiality, or Christ's equality with the Father. This was an attempt to refute Arianism, which said Christ was only a creature subordinate to the Father.

(2) **The First Council of Constantinople** (381 A.D.) defended the reality of a human soul in Jesus. This disputes a heresy known as Appolinarianism.

(3) **The Council of Ephesus** (431 A.D.) fought Nestorianism; which taught that there were two persons in Christ, human and divine, and that Mary was only the mother of the human. Ephesus stressed that Christ was one person with two natures.

(4) **The Council of Chalcedon** (451 A.D.) reiterated a rejection of Nestorianism and also tackled monophysitism, which taught Christ had only one nature, the divine.

(5) **The Second Council of Constantinople** (533 A.D.) reiterated the Church's condemnation of Nestorianism and monophysitism.

(6) **The Third Council of Constantinople** (581 A.D.) refuted nontheletism, which taught Christ had only one will. The Council said that two wills were operative in Christ, the human and the divine.

(7) **The Fourth Council of Lateran** (1295), the **Council of Lyons** (1274), the **Council of Florence** (1442), and the **Council of Trent** (1547–1563) all reiterated previous Christological statements and formulas.

Besides the works of ancient Christian antiquity and the pronouncements of Councils, other individuals have significantly shaped our beliefs about Jesus Christ. St. Augustine, after a rakish young adulthood and a profound conversion, developed a depraved understanding of human nature and popularized the notion of original sin—that is, that all human beings are born in the clutches of evil. Christ is our mediator with God, who can free us from the chains of original sin, and Christ claims individuals for freedom and God through the Sacrament of Baptism. Anselm popularized the theory of satisfaction, that only a God–man could pay the debt owed to God because of the sin of Adam. Thomas Aquinas reflects an increasingly metaphysical discussion of Jesus Christ. His work reaffirms the decisions of previous Councils and goes on to emphasize the union of two natures in one person, the functioning of the human and divine wills in Christ, His powers, and His consciousness. Aquinas's theology epitomizes the "Christ in Himself" direction of theologizing, almost putting Christ under a metaphysical microscope and analyzing Him.

In the background is a "Christ-for-us" approach, an approach experienced by the evangelizers and early Christians and to which we have returned to in recent decades. Medieval and post-medieval thought traditionally emphasized the mysteries of the incarnation and redemption, often with the emphasis (in the latter) being on the atoning death of Jesus. It was not until the 1960s that renewed emphasis was placed on the resurrection of Christ as the centerpiece of redemption.

We have witnessed in recent decades a shift from high Christology (heavily philosophical, metaphysical) to a low Christology, or a Christology "from below." Such an approach is much more existential, stressing the impact or difference Jesus makes in personal and communal living without denying the mystery and ontological dimensions of Christ. Elizabeth Johnson in *Consider Jesus* sees a contemporary turning point to be a 1951 commemorative essay written by Karl Rahner, entitled "Chalcedon: End or Beginning?" In it, Rahner contended that Christology was stagnant in the Church since it was not claiming the passion or conviction of the people of God. Essentially, he saw not much progress in our understanding of Jesus in 1500 years. Richard McBrien in *Catholicism, Volume One,* mentions a little attended-to work, *The Resurrection* by Francis X. Durwell, also as a turning point. Durwell is the theologian in modern times who retrieved the resurrection as the centerpiece of the redemptive event. In modern times, Rahner, Hans Küng, Walter Kasper, Edward Schillebeeckx, and more recently Rosemary Radford Ruether, Elizabeth Schüssler Fiorenza, Monika Hellwig, Elizabeth Johnson, and other feminist theologians, have restored emphasis on Christ's resurrection, Christ as the revelation of God, the creator and Parent, and Jesus' personal mission regarding the Kingdom of God. Teilhard de Chardin and Piet Schoonenberg, in their work, have placed the Christ event in an evolutionary process sort of context. Leonardo Boff is a beacon in another movement, liberation theology, stressing that the Jesus of history stood for the transformation of reality and history. For Boff and others, the Jesus of history is more vital and experiential than the ontological Christ of faith.

The discussion of the historically evolving Christ would be incomplete without at least mentioning Protestant contributions. The work of Rudolf Bultmann has certainly contributed toward interest in Jesus' mission and ministry regarding the Kingdom of God, and offered people an existential, life-changing experience of Jesus. He stressed the Jesus that people experience in faith, and said the Jesus of history was impossible to recover. A particular favorite of mine has been Paul Tillich. In his three volumes of *Systematic Theology, The Courage to Be,* and other writings, Tillich speaks of the New Being, a state of renewed being ushered in by Jesus' resurrection, and the courage that comes from union with Jesus' New Being. This courage bridges the chasms created by the sin, anxiety, and estrangement in the world.

In *The Cost of Discipleship* and other writings, Dietrich Bonhoeffer critiqued the church for being agents of cheap grace, with little or no discernible conversion going on in Protestant and Catholic congregations in Europe in the mid-twentieth century. He crafted an image of Jesus as the servant, the person for others, and called those who claim to be Christian to follow the master's example.

John O'Grady performed a great service for students of Christology in his 1981 *Models of Jesus.* Much like Avery Dulles did in *Models of Church,* O'Grady summarizes the major blocks of material that have evolved theologically and spiritually. For the last two thousand years, Jesus Christ has been for believers:

(1) the second person of the Trinity, an image that provides us with doctrinal security and clarity;

(2) the Man for others, or model person—the One like whom we are to become;

(3) the ethical liberator of liberation theologians and all who believe God's reign involves the transformation of society;

(4) the mythological Christ (a la Bultmann) whose historicity is irrelevant—the stories of this Christ are valuable for the meaning they offer us;

(5) Jesus, the personal savior, perhaps the most exciting model of Jesus—this is the Jesus who saves, rescues, redeems us from our personal sin and chaos;

(6) Jesus, the human face of God, or the revelation of the mystery of God.

Though all of the models of Jesus form a synthetic whole of the experience of Jesus down through the centuries, and though each of the models has intrinsic strengths and weaknesses, O'Grady believes "the human face of God" to be the most Scripturally accurate.

Conversion:
Goal of Pastoral Ministry

*I*n a recent article, Msgr. Robert Fuller, a vicar in the
diocese of Tucson, Arizona, and one of the pioneers in
the RENEW movement, lamented that "our parishes are
failing." The failure, he says, lies in the fact that parishes
are not helping people in the process of conversion, spiritual
transformation, and life change. We have just devoted a considerable amount of space and time discussing the mission
of Jesus, namely, ushering in God's Kingdom, or God's
Reign. The goal of contemporary evangelization is to invite
people to the Kingdom, to Kingdom living. Another way of
describing the Kingdom or God's Reign is God breaking into
a person's life. These breakdowns that become break-
throughs are frequently called conversion experiences. Parishes exist to help foster and facilitate conversion to the
Kingdom.

Conversion happens in and through human experiences.
Just as God called Moses in Exodus, chapter 3, to a new
direction through the burning bush, so also God in our own
day is using contemporary burning bushes to call people to
his Reign. What are some of the human moments or events
that can become thresholds for conversion? Among them
are:

- falling in love
- a relationship falling apart
- significant loss
- sickness or physical suffering
- job or financial difficulties
- emotional distress and suffering
- addiction

The list goes on and on. Any human experience can become a threshold experience for meeting God. The *felt* experiences involved in typical conversion processes are many. They include: ache, struggle, inner wrestling, loneliness, despair, voiding out, feelings of dislocation, grief, anxiety, and ultimately letting go, surrendering into a new experience of God's power, grace, and Reign. Though the experience is human, ordinary, the person involved definitely feels he or she has encountered the Holy One. In effect, what "jumps" in a conversion moment is the imagination. The imagination is the synthesis of a person's intuitions, feelings, thoughts, and physical senses. In conversion experiences the imagination "jumps" to God.

Paul Tillich wrote years ago about what we speak of as a particular time or moment when we consciously surrendered to or felt God. Tillich maintained that often what we refer to as our conversion experience is rather a moment of high awareness in a process of events and experiences that constitute the actual conversion. Often much is going on underground in a person's psyche, deep memory, imagination, and value system that leads up to a moment of high consciousness or awareness, the conversion experience.

We need also to be cautious regarding superficial conversions or false conversions. These have abounded in recent years in at least some pockets of evangelical religions. Writing in *Turning to Christ* some years ago, Urban Holmes lamented that some of the "quickie" conversions, often manipulated out of people through the rote repetition of the sinner's prayer, are exactly that: false or superficial conversions. Holmes warned that we ought to be cautious about any form of evangelization— conversion efforts that result in people saying they have no problems because of the power of Christ in their lives, or that they no longer wrestle with sin or the forces of evil because of their conversion. Such approaches amount to the denial of both reality and the presence of a deep memory that in many of us leaves scar tissue which is not removed by conversion.

I saw a young man recently in a one-on-one setting. He was seeking my counsel and advice. He talked about his lucrative job, his comfortable middle-class lifestyle, his nice home. But he said despite all this security, he was asking himself a recurring question: "Is this all there is? Is this what adulthood is about: money, job, routine?" He went on to say that he felt a profound loneliness in his life—that his relationships were inadequate, that there was no one "special" in his life. Indeed, most of his relationships were with "drinking buddies," with whom intimacy was impossible. He also reported feeling a great distance between himself and God and the church.

I told this young man that though he felt far from God and church, I felt he was going through a conversion process. I told him of John Walsh, the pioneering Maryknoll missionary in the work of evangelization. Walsh has taught for years that there is no true conversion until a person has articulated two "primal cries." The first is the "primal cry for more"— a hunger for God, for the transcendent. The young man's perception of the superficiality of his creature comforts amounted to just this—a cry for more. In addition, his quest to penetrate loneliness and experience intimacy falls into the category of Walsh's "primal cry for help," or existential awareness that one cannot do life alone, but indeed needs others, needs community. What does conversion look like? It is an often painful experience of "crying for more" and "crying for help."

One day in class at an Institute where I was teaching, I asked a group of graduate students in ministry to discern and mention their gifts, their charisms. Most of the middle-aged students jumped immediately to listing their gifts of doing and having. One student, a young woman directly out of college, in her first graduate course, surprised the class by saying that her greatest gift was the syndrome of clinical depression that she had suffered from for several years. I asked her to explain that a bit, and she explained that "the cross" of her depression had become a gift that sensitized her to the suffering of others and made her more sympathetic to the ache in others' lives. Her depression led her to ministry, to help others in the healing process, as she had been helped through the faith and ministry of others. Conversion involves a kind of paradoxical thinking and feeling, in which one begins to intuit, as my young student did, that a cross can become a gift, a blessing. Indeed most of us have wounded-ness out of which we operate, and which has made us more sensitive in our relationships, and for some of us, in our ministry.

Recently I went through a difficult bout with an illness. The sickness caused me to take off work for weeks, a particular crisis for a compulsive workaholic. One night I desperately needed sacred space for reflection and prayer. I drove for a considerable time, seeking out a Catholic church in which I might pray. I found none open. All were locked, probably because of the danger in the Chicago area of vandalism. I drove by a Lutheran church, however, and stopped. I found its doors open for would-be seekers. I went in, opened a copy of the New Testament, and began to pray the psalms. I was truly troubled, my spirit feeling like I had come to the end of the road, the end of my ministry. As I prayed, and wept, I looked up into the sanctuary area. Two banners were hanging before me. On the left side of the sanctuary there was one banner that read "Become a New Creation!" Next to that was the crucifix, the price or cost of discipleship. And next to the cross, on the right of the sanctuary, there was another banner that read "All Things Can Be Made New in Christ!" I closed the Bible, stood, and praised God, praised God for speaking to me, revealing and manifesting himself to me through the banners. God did not make the banners; God did not hang the banners. But God spoke powerfully through them, that I was not at a dead end, but at a new beginning, at a turn in the road.

What happened in that Lutheran church that night? Revelation happened! How does revelation, itself a conversion experience, happen? It happens through the firing of the imagination. The imagination is the synthesis, the convergence of intellect, physical senses, and emotions. Conversion is the jumping of the imagination to new dominant images, in this case from the imagery of despair and hopelessness, to the hopeful imagery of the Kingdom, God's Reign.

I was in a large archdiocese in the United States doing a weekend of renewal for a parish on the occasion of the dedication of their renewed sanctuary area. As I was processing with the group of parishioners, one of them asked my opinion about a current situation with the bishop of the archdiocese. The bishop was to come the following week to dedicate the renovation formally. But he sent word ahead that at this special celebration, no women were to serve as eucharistic ministers, nor were women to be in the sanctuary area at all. What ensued was a long conversation about codependency with a dysfunctional institution and prophetic confrontation with that institution. About an hour into the conversation, a man stood up and said the following: "I have been away from the Catholic Church for twenty-five years. I came to this day of renewal in the hope of experiencing something new. But I can tell you that as a church, you are the same kind of infantized navel-gazers that I left years ago. For you to take seriously the mandate of a sexist prelate as you have been doing is unacceptable. Did your sanctuary in fact need renovation? I think if Jesus were physically present, he would have trouble with both the renovation and the institution's stance toward women. Why, I think he might gut your sanctuary and turn it into a shelter for the hungry and the homeless. Look outside this place; there are people sleeping under cardboard in the park! Do you think Jesus would care about all this churchy stuff with that going on outside?" With that, the man and the woman with him stood and exited the church hall, apparently leaving his church of origin for the second time.

An overreaction on his part? Perhaps so! But the whole uncomfortable scenario reminded me of a core truth: that conversion is incomplete without a sensitivity to and commitment to the work of social justice. Pope Paul VI said this clearly in *Evangelii nuntiandi* when he spoke of evangelization as the transformation of society with the power of the gospel. Jim Wallis, of the *Sojourners* community and magazine, in his book *The Call to Conversion* says that true conversion necessitates proximity to the victims of social injustice, proximity in the sense of physical presence or at least education of and informing one's self about social issues and social justice. Wallis says another needed factor is to pray for people and issues involved in social-justice concerns and ministry. We need to carry these people and their issues in our hearts prayerfully. We need to include them also in our communal prayer or worship. Prayer literally changes our hearts and melts our indifference to the suffering of others.

Conversion: it involves the cry for more, the cry for help, paradoxical thinking and feeling, jumping imaginations, and increased social-justice consciousness.

We have not yet mentioned one dynamic that is constitutive to conversion. Why is it that some people have the kind of human experiences that I have mentioned and they experience conversion, while other people become agnostic or atheistic, or some turn to contemporary forms of idolatry? Edward Braxton, in his book *The Wisdom Community*, highlights the importance of community in facilitating conversion experiences. The community might take the form of one person who represents the community and tradition—a pastoral counselor, a spiritual director, a neighbor, a friend, a relative. Or the community might be represented by a small group, a small community or a program or organization or ministry at church. But it is being with people of faith, conversation, and prayer that helps an individual take the leap of faith that is conversion, to begin to trust, hope, surrender, and experience God and community in a new, fresh way. Community is the context, the agency through which conversion happens. Worship or liturgy is the culture that fosters conversion. We come to one another and worship with one another with the intuition, "I think I have met God through human experience. I think I heard the voice of God in a contemporary burning bush." Community is the source of confirmation that indeed we have met God. It is hard to "grow" as a Christian without community.

This raises a central pastoral issue addressed throughout the rest of this book. The People of God are having burning-bush conversion experiences with great frequency. What is absent in Catholic culture is sufficient quantitative and qualitative pastoral presence to these potential conversion moments. The People of God are falling through the cracks for want of effective pastoring. This is because the pastoring function is still relegated to the male cleric and his often minimal staff. It is mythic, in the worse sense of the term, to think a handful of professionals can pastor the thousands of potential members in our parishes. The pastoring function needs to be shared with the baptized who are willing to come forward for training and formation.

Finally, we need to avoid the naive view that there is some kind of univocal, uniform conversion experience that people go through. People in our parishes and institutions are "all over the lot." Some are awakening to the "mystery," others to a personal God. Some are experiencing conversion to Jesus Christ as Lord. Others are hearing the call to ecclesial conversion or a new appreciation of church. Some are experiencing moral conversion, or the pull to put the gospel into action and turn from sin. Others are experiencing intellectual conversion, holding on to the truth of their church of origin, while recognizing the truth and wisdom of other cultures and faith traditions.

Those of us committed to the work of evangelization and conversion need to grow in an attitude of comfort toward chaos. Chaos was indeed the primal experience of church. That which was experienced as wind and fire in Acts 2 came to be named Holy Spirit.

Toward Original Wholeness and Communion

There are various levels of meaning conveyed by the creation accounts in Genesis: the nature of sin, the need for redemption, the nature of creation, and others. An intriguing one is Yahweh God's insight in Genesis 2:18: "It is not good that man should be alone." God's plan for the human family seems to be relationship, oneness, community, at root—communion. The human family was created for "union with . . . " one another and ultimately God. The presumption in this statement is that there is a kind of primal unity that we have been made for and which God calls us to, that is unity with ourselves. Psychotherapists might call this congruence with the self, philosophers and ethicists might call it integrity. The church has traditionally called it holiness. Before we can become one with others and God, there needs to be at least in process a quest for wholeness within one's self.

Wholeness is a convergence of realities. Wholeness is happening when a person is working on one's physical, emotional, spiritual well-being. With such a quest in process, one begins to intuit the incompleteness of the self, the need for connections with other humans and the need also for connectedness with an ultimate ground of being, God. In the Christian tradition, it is said that we are made in the image and likeness of God. God is Trinity, three in one. God is many yet one. God is communion. If we are made in God's image, we are many, yet made for wholeness and communion. Our existential Trinitarian experience is that individuals in the process of wholeness are called, indeed gravitate toward, further unity with others and God. There is an underground river in the human psyche and soul. It is the power, the current pulling us toward communion.

But there is an undertow in that underground river. It has been named sin, idolatry, alienation, original sin. The objective fact is that we have a powerful tendency to choose "apples" over communion. God's will or plan for us is communion. In paradise, Adam and Eve in the Genesis myth feel no shame regarding their nakedness. After disobeying God's will and eating forbidden fruit, they feel shame. They run from God. Once caught and confronted by God, they experience further alienation as they blame each other and eventually the serpent for their disobedient, self-focused choices and behavior.

Genesis 2 is the story of paradise lost. The Kingdom/Reign of God in the preaching and ministry of Jesus, discussed in chapter 1, is Jesus' attempt to achieve paradise restored. God's Reign is redemption, salvation. The plan of God, the will of God for Trinitarian lives of communion, was put back on track with the life, death, and Resurrection of Jesus. But despite the victory of Easter over sin, suffering, and death, we are not out of the garden scene yet. The power of the Resurrection, uniting the entire cosmos in and through the risen Christ, has yet to be fully actualized. It is the work of the followers of Jesus to more fully expand the effects of the victory, lives of communion, moving toward total communion

and glory in eternity. God's Reign begins here and extends
through the veil of death into eternal life.

The forces of divisiveness are still powerfully at work in
the universe. From the time of Christ to our own day, the
need for power, aggression, wealth, individualism, and mis-
guided independence have caused wars, injustice, martyrdom, and a consistent breakdown of the relational. In our
own day, this alienation and separation has insidiously moved
into the sacred space traditionally held by the nuclear family.
Families and homes are divided over confusion of gender
roles and divorce. Writing in *The Seven Habits of Highly
Effective People*, Stephen Covey laments that the great mistake of modern people is to equate maturity with independence. Covey says independence is only the second step on
a continuum toward maturity. Maturity is had in moving
from the dependence of a child to the independence of an
adolescent to that of adulthood.

Unfortunately the church, called by Christ to participate
in the redemption of society, has done little more than echo
the mistaken values and structures of society in its structures
and governance systems. At a recent graduate class on evangelization at an institute on pastoral issues, I was making a
presentation on what I consider to be at least some of the
heart-values we must adhere to if we are to do evangelization
on the parish level. Heart-values are core values or attitudes,
heartfelt convictions that precede strategizing or structuring
for mission. I said that a community serious about evangelization must

   (1) begin with needs, listen to people's needs, listen to
      and try to understand their woundedness;

   (2) plan ministries and programs that address these real-
      life needs (these first two heart-values are essentially
      the posture of preevangelization);

(3) through preaching, religious education efforts, and faith-formation experiences, clearly and with consistency present, proclaim the message, the good news of God's Reign;

(4) facilitate multiple opportunities for people to meet or re-meet Jesus, and the God of Jesus (conversion);

(5) provide relational support for the journey of conversion; ideally these take the shape of small groups or communities, the emerging paradigm for future church;

(6) in such a communal setting, teach parishioners how to connect the richness of Scripture, the tradition of the church, and life experience, resulting, hopefully, in intuitions of revelation, God's self-manifesting in ordinary experience;

(7) through the mutual ministries of the liturgical assembly, provide meaningful liturgical moments, worship, that brings the message and the presence of God home, into people's souls, hearts, imaginations; good liturgy is a mosaic of charisms and ministries converging, synergizing that both expresses the faith of a community and actually forms the community;

(8) through workshops and spiritual direction train people in the skills of discernment of charisms;

(9) engage in the deeply spiritual activity of ministerial training, unleashing the power of a community for *diakonia* that flows from each member's Baptism;

(10) commission and send forth people of discernment, and trained baptismal ministers, to lives of stewardship, that is, the wise use of one's charisms for the

common good and the glory of God (only a small part of stewardship involves concern about financial resources);

(11) in line with sending forth for stewardship, help people grow in the skills of critical awareness regarding the dominant images and values of the consumer culture we live in, that adults and young people might better name which are of Christ and the Reign of God and which are antithetical to gospel living (evangelization, wrote Bernard Häring in *Evangelization Today*, must become a movement toward morality, toward the discernment of what is right, good, the truth);

(12) help people re-imagine their life's work as participation in the cocreation of the world and the Kingdom of God; instill in people a sense of vocation regarding their jobs, that their goal in work is not just for profit, but rather bringing Christ and God's Reign into the marketplace.

When I finished the presentation, one student was in support of these needed heart-values for an organization committed to evangelizing. She earnestly asked, however, how the church had gotten so far from them. Perhaps my response was an overgeneralization, but I suggested that with Constantine's merging the state and Christianity, the church early in its history had been "taken in by society."

Rather then being a countercultural force for change, the church did little more that sprinkle holy water on structures of power and aggression. These have become the hierarchical, sexist, clerical governance systems of the church. Along with the structures is an ecclesiology, a vision of church, supposedly given to us by God, through Christ, that says this top-down power model is divine will, immutable, not to be questioned, never to be changed.

Gerald Arbuckle, in *Re-Founding the Church,* suggests that the ecclesiological and structural paradigm paralysis that the church is in runs the risk of growing worse as we approach a new millennium. Those in authority seem to be in a posture of restorationism, trying to return the church to a pre-Vatican II vision and praxis. When Arbuckle calls for the refounding of the church, and the protection of rather than the witch-hunting and outlawing of refounding leaders within the church, he is advocating two realities. First of all, he is calling for a rebeginning of the church, a new beginning around evangelization. In speaking of evangelization, he is not advocating a universal program of bean counting, playing the numbers game regarding how many people we are getting to church. No, his call is for communities, the church universal becoming much more focused on what we discussed in this book so far: What did Jesus mean by God's Reign, how can we live that reality, how does conversion happen? Is God's will that we be in communion, in communities? How do we do that? His second admonition is that we begin to imagine and create innovative strategies and structures of mission and ministry that fit the mission of God's Reign and the quest for conversion. Such new strategies would necessitate letting other antiquated, ineffective strategies die, grieving them, and moving on to new models and paradigms. Many in the church refuse that grieving process and, in effect, stifle the Spirit and block the rebirth of the church. "I tell you that the Kingdom of God will be taken from you and given to people who will produce its proper fruit" (Matt. 21:43). Jesus' warning is cutting today as people gravitate to recovery groups, Twelve Step meetings, and other therapeutic movements because their church of origin is more concerned about maintenance of the status quo than the mission given us by Jesus.

Enabling the Empowered

*P*erhaps it is jargon or hairsplitting, but I recurrently take issue with people, in the public forum, when I hear them speaking of the need for the clergy to empower the laity. Speaking as a priest, I cannot empower anyone. God empowers. And God's people are empowered already. I have become a firm believer in the presence of gifts of the Holy Spirit, charisms in each person. I have become convinced of the need for better and more efforts at helping people discern what their gifts are. Ministry is using one's gifts to help advance the cause of, facilitate the coming of God's Reign, the Kingdom of God. Such ministry can certainly take place in the context of church or parish-based ministry. But ministry needs also to take place in the domestic church of one's primary relationships. And, as has already been noted, the greatest challenge is to reframe one's life's work as the possibility of cocreating the world with God, bringing Christ and the values of the gospel to the marketplace, ushering in God's Reign.

At several parishes with whom I have consulted over the past ten years, discernment of charisms is being taken seriously. At its Ministries Conference, the North American Forum on the Catechumenate encourages catechumenal teams not just to divide up the tasks involved in initiation, but rather as a team to discern giftedness and to try to effect a good marriage between needs and gifts.

While discernment must be the basic stance and approach of a faith community in general, I have also found it valuable to use the celebration of Pentecost to give the entire worshiping congregation a taste of what discernment of gifts of the Spirit is all about. For years, at St. John the Evangelist in Streamwood, Illinois, the staff would alert the community about the ministerial needs of the parish. The celebration of Pentecost became, then, a call to discernment and to the mission of the Kingdom. The weeks after Pentecost were filled with discernment opportunities for those who felt called or were just interested in some ministry.

Attempting discernment is an attempt to get beyond ministry as volunteerism, as well as beyond the parish as a collection of programs and organizations. To use the words of pastoral theologian John de Beers, discernment is the threshold to baptismal ministry, service that flows from the dignity and responsibility of being baptized into the Body of Christ.

The steps of discernment can be made quite simple. I have used a model like the one that follows in several parishes, as well as in groups at conferences and institutes.

(1) Encourage people to listen to themselves and their lives. This is best done in silence, alone in a nearby room, chapel, taking a walk, etc. The reflection questions are essentially How has God gifted me? What are my gifts of doing, or abilities that I have that can be used for the common good and the glory of God? What are my gifts of being, that is, who am I as a person? What qualities, values, attributes do I possess that can be put at the service of the common good and also that can be used to glorify God?

(2) After this initial listening, the discerning person returns to a group from his or her parish or organization. All have engaged in the listening session. Now each person takes a turn, sharing with the group the gifts of doing and being that the individual has found in the self.

(3) The group, which knows the individual, responds to each speaker, supporting the individual's discernment, in some cases gently challenging it and in some cases giving the individual/speaker new insights into his or her giftedness, pointing out gifts perhaps not previously seen.

Discernment is a key step in moving toward an enabled, empowered congregation. In addition to discernment another key element is the re-imagination of staff roles, including that of pastor. Many of us who are staff members in parishes were agents of direct delivery. The ordained, those with professional training, delivered services to the laity. In the proposed model, "the professionals" take on the role of animators and trainers. The personal discipline that I operate out of is as follows:

The *ordained* (professional credentialed) work with *lay leaders* who coordinate *communities of ministers* who serve a given *target group* of the faith community, who have expressed some need awaiting a pastoral response and ministry.

One of the many functions of the lay leader of a ministering community is to encourage discernment, so that the many gifts within a small group might be harnessed in addressing the target group and the discerned needs. Several comments are needed here for clarification.

I prefer to speak of communities of ministers. I choose the word *communities* very deliberately. The word says a lot more than team, council, or board. Before even getting to a given ministerial activity, a ministering community prays together, discusses Scripture together, and shares life and life stories. Thus, any ministerial tasks are rooted in rich soil. This is quite different from a volunteer-activities approach to ministry, in which a person performs a given function for a parish but operates pretty much alone. Communities of ministers operate collaboratively.

Training, which largely is done by a re-imagined staff, is a profoundly spiritual activity. Training is no less than this: the full unleashing of the gifts of the Holy Spirit present in a congregation. Ministerial training ought to take 50 to 75 percent of a staff's time, if the staff is truly enabling. The area in which the staff trains is based on their own expertise and areas of giftedness. Most of my ministry has been involved in evangelization, the broader field of religious education, and counseling. These are the areas in which I teach and train in the School of Ministry we have in the parish I am currently involved with, Holy Family in Inverness, Illinois.

For those areas of ministerial training in which no staff member has expertise or competence, consultants from outside the parish can be brought in, or to better cover expenses, parishes that are contiguous can network in bringing a resource person. As of this writing, Holy Family is consulting with a neighboring parish about doing some School of Ministry sessions together.

These comments are being written from the perspective of parishes that are structured to offer general services to the parish at large. I personally believe that the emerging paradigm for parish is that of a network of small groups and communities. In that emerging model, ministerial training will still be needed. But I believe the focus of ministering will change. No longer will people go to programs or organizations for ministry to happen to them or be done to them.

In the future, the essential ministries of religious education, worship, pastoral care, youth ministry will be done, at least in part, within the boundaries of the natural group or community. Within the small intentional group, the same principles of enablement, discernment, and training will be even more essential. The future of the church and the importance of small groups and communities will be discussed in other chapters of this book.

Toward the Communal Parish

*I*t is evident to most people in church work that the old paradigm of parish life, that which consists mostly of programs and organizations with clergy and professional staff doing direct delivery, is dysfunctional and is no longer effective. What is not clear to many people is what the *new* paradigm is or what it will look like. Yet there seems to be a growing consensus that the key ingredient of the new paradigm has something to do with community or communion, with people united with one another and God.

The scriptural roots of the new paradigm can be found in Acts 2. At the birth of the church, the key ingredients that I see are these: the power of the Holy Spirit is experienced as fire and wind. Wind and fire are not a program or organizations. Wind and fire are usually associated with chaos. The church was born in chaos. That chaotic, powerful Holy Spirit prompted Peter to evangelize. Peter gave a bold, kerygmatic proclamation of who Jesus was: how Jesus was crucified, but how death could not keep a hold on him; how Jesus, through the power of God, experienced the victory of the Resurrection. Peter's evangelization turned a crowd of anonymous people into a community of spiritual seekers. People listening to Peter asked him, "What are we to do?" Peter responded with a very incisive answer. He said that the people must change their lives and be baptized. We can discern from this line a core value of the early church: initiation, ritual, and the early forms of the sacraments were always joined to life-change, joined to conversion. Sacraments had not yet become what they would in the medieval period— holy things that people took at a culturally appropriate time.

We hear also from Luke's Acts 2 some other important sacramental praxis. So many people in our day experience sacramental moments as graduation time. A sacrament is the last contact a person has with the church until the next time a holy thing is to be received. Luke tells us that those who were to be baptized devoted themselves to the *communal life*. He goes on to tell us what the communal life looked like. They went to the *temple* daily. They also met in *one another's homes* for the breaking of the bread and prayer and the apostle's instruction.

How was ministry done? It was not done by an elite core who had been trained or who had gone to a seminary. All shared their goods in common based on their gifts. There was a marriage in the early church between needs and gifts. There was a spirit of stewardship. Much evangelization happened by contagion. That particular passage of Luke, Acts 2, closes with the statement "day by day the Lord added to their number." The statement seems to suggest that there was a magnetic force attracting people to Christianity. There was not much payoff for becoming a Christian besides persecution and death. But there was a passion about the community that was magnetic and attractive. Evangelization happened by contagion.

So what was the church like at its birth? It was a chaotic experience. The chaos led to evangelization. Evangelization prompted conversion, which was celebrated in sacramental ritual. Conversion and ritual led to the communal life. The communal life was further characterized by stewardship and ministry. Ministry was characterized by the marriage of gifts and needs. Evangelization was not a program but a contagious, passionate attitude.

It seems to me that the Holy Spirit is moving us back in the direction of the first days of the church. It seems to me the emerging paradigm of future church is that of *community*. In this chapter we will explore this emerging paradigm, which is vital for what evangelization will look like in the future church.

The communal model or image of church has always been of special interest to me. Even in my college and graduate-school years, I had the growing feeling that parishes were run ineffectively. I sensed even then that good pastoral care was not taking place in our parishes. Living in the Archdiocese of Chicago as I have all my life, I have been part of large parishes—some with several thousand units or households. It always seemed strange to me, especially when there was not a clergy shortage, that there might be two, three, or four associate pastors and other staff members and they would be centralized at the parish plant. I had a growing feeling that pastoral leadership ought to be decentralized. I felt that parish leadership ought to move more and more out to the grassroots, to be with the people. I remember wondering some twenty-five years ago, reflecting on my own parish, St. Thomas More, which had two associates, why isn't the pastoring function broken up in three ways? Why isn't this large parish broken up into three sections? Why doesn't the support staff go with each of the priests to create miniparishes within the context of the large parish? That seminal dream began to become actualized in my first assignment at St. Hubert parish, Hoffman Estates, Illinois. For the first four years of my tenure there as associate pastor and director of religious education, I operated very much out of the old paradigm of programs and organizations. I was coordinating programs for literally thousands of people, most of whom were sending their children to catechetical programs.

Over 50 percent of families enrolled in our programs were single-parent families or blended families. In the 1970s the family had already begun to crumble; the clan had began to decay. Most folks, in terms of sacramental catechesis or sacramental praxis, were chasing after "holy things," usually for their children. These people showed little interest in what Luke called in Acts 2 "the communal life." Then in the late 1970s, the staff of St. Hubert's began to experiment with a new form of parish. During Lent of 1977, we invited the entire parish and representative parishioners from sections of the parish to six Monday evenings of reflection and renewal, during which we reflected on the state of our parish and the future of parish life. We began with about 350 people, and by the end of Lent still had about 150 to 160 people who were deeply interested and invested in the process. The conversations that we had with these people, people from the grassroots of parish life, were very revealing. People who stayed with the process said that they experienced the parish as too big, too cold, too anonymous. They were hungering for parish experiences of a more communal nature.

That Lenten program led to an expansive effort that we called "Neighborhood Ministry." Neighborhood Ministry existed on several levels. Throughout the parish we trained neighborhood ministers who were, in effect, home visitors. Equipping them with human-relations skills, we commissioned them to visit their fellow parishioners, especially the inactive and the shut-in, on a regular basis. These neighborhood ministers became research experts in the field, reporting back to the staff what was going on in the real life of the parish. As I have said in other publications, this reach-out component, the messenger, as he or she is called by the Movement for a Better World, is a difficult role requiring ongoing training and support. In addition to this reach-out role, we also began to offer regular experiences of small group gatherings.

If I were to critique these early experiences, I would have to say they were too clerical or priest-bound. Quite often people wanted a priest to come out and lead a prayer service or preside at Mass. At the time, I thought it was worthwhile to engage in this priest-bound effort, to get the movement off the ground to facilitate people meeting in one another's homes. People would at least talk about the Gospel from a Mass that we celebrated together. They would talk and pray with one another. Many home Masses then gave birth to small groups who met around catechetical materials that the coordinating group suggested.

A very positive, well-received result of the Lenten experience were neighborhood social events. People gathered in streets, in one another's backyards for neighborhood picnics, barbecues, and family gatherings. We were moving, during those years at St. Hubert's, toward a communal model of parish. But something was brought to my attention by someone who was serving as coordinator of neighborhood ministry at the time, a layman in the parish, Gordon LaBounty. Gordon pointed out to me one day that we had begun to create two parallel parishes. He said that on the one hand, we had the old organization—a program parish whose activities were coordinated by the various boards of the parish. But, he said, we had another parish emerging—the neighborhood-oriented, communal model. Gordon commented that we did not have enough energy to run both kinds of parishes. We had to move in one direction or the other. In terms of leadership, he noted, we were burning people out. Some of the same people were leading/serving in both the program church and also in the neighborhood-communal church.

I thought Gordon's comments were on target. However, his comments and all the hard work that went into neighborhood ministry occurred at the end of my tenure at St. Hubert's. I moved on to St. Albert the Great. Gordon tried to continue the efforts that we had initiated toward a communal model of parish. But with a changing staff over the years, with a vision different from the one that we shared, Gordon with little support found it difficult to continue. He went on to experience community in a new way, in an effort begun at St. Hubert's called "Kingdom weekends."

The effect of the Kingdom weekends was similar to our efforts at neighborhood ministry. Folks who experienced the retreat later went on for training and formation and subsequently become leaders of the next retreat. It is my assessment of the Kingdom weekends and other such models that they are not necessarily contributing to the shift that is needed for a new model or a new paradigm for parish. Those who experienced the intense community experience of the weekends often became an "elite," people who had "done" the weekends. But their presence and experience did not contribute to the conversion of parish systems.

In 1980, I transferred to St. Albert the Great, where I became both associate pastor and director of religious education. St. Albert's, in Burbank, Illinois, was and is a quite different parish from those in Chicago's northwest suburbs. It sits on the border of the city and the southwest suburbs, resembling a Chicago neighborhood more than a suburb. Many parishioners are blue-collar workers with a need for at least two paychecks coming into the home. St. Albert's demographics are older in nature than those of St. Hubert's.

The average age of a parishioner at the time of my assignment there was about forty-five. Many parishioners had moved to this area to escape some of the upheavals of urban and racial-ethnic change in the center city. It was my mistake to think that I could transplant neighborhood ministry, the role of neighborhood ministers, and our style of small groups at St. Hubert's to this more conservative, slow-to-change area of the archdiocese. My initial attempts at small communities at St. Albert the Great were ineffective. I was trying to replicate a previous success within a quite different cultural milieu.

One day I had a flash of insight, or perhaps a conversion experience, regarding my struggles at St. Albert's. One day as I was walking out of church after celebrating Mass, I had to step over the legs of a man kneeling on a cold, hard linoleum floor, praying before a statue of Mary. At first I was annoyed by the man's devotionalism, but as I stared at him, several things occurred to me. I realized I did not yet love the people of that parish; I did not love them in their devotionalism. I was reminded of Paul VI's words in *Evangelii nuntiandi*, that there can be no effective evangelization if the evangelizer does not love the people he or she is evangelizing. Evangelization needs to be an act of love. I had not yet accepted these people and their style of spirituality. I was reminded of Paul VI's further admonition that evangelization efforts have to begin where people are at—often with their devotionalism.

The people in Burbank, Illinois, were and are devotional people. The man kneeling before Mary's statue that morning led me to the conviction that, if small communities were to take off in this parish, it would have to be through the people's devotionalism.

As the next Advent approached, I asked a carpenter friend of mine if he could make for the parish a replica of the

manger that Christ was placed in at his birth. The man
constructed a manger, placed some straw in it, and presented it to me. I advertised in the bulletin and from the
pulpit, after consulting with the emerging liturgical leaders,
that the Advent theme that year was to be "Christ can be
reborn in our hearts." I asked anyone who wished to host
the traveling manger in their home for a neighborhood
prayer service or Mass to call the rectory to register. People
rushed to respond. We could not accommodate all who
called in, willing to offer their homes and also to reach out
to others to invite them to their homes. The prayer services
and Masses filled people's living rooms. Much as people
did at St. Hubert's, here in their own devotional style the
parishioners would reflect on the seasonal Scriptures. People proactively invited neighbors, friends, and coworkers
into their homes.

Because of the success of the Advent experience, I offered
another series of home gatherings during Lent, this time
around a traveling cross. We had similar success. In evaluat-
ing these two devotional seasons of Advent and Lent, those
of us working on the project discerned that these devotional-
communal efforts were the preevangelization needed to ac-
quaint people with a different style of being church. The
following year, St. Albert's began a two and one-half year
journey via the RENEW materials. RENEW dramatically
changed the fiber and timber of St. Albert the Great.
Though there have been staff and personnel changes and
struggles over the years, people have more and more become aware and comfortable with the communal model of
church.

I stayed at St. Albert the Great for only two years. My
next assignment was at St. Michael's in Orland Park on the
farthest southwest corner of the archdiocese. I stayed at St.
Michael's for eleven years. My efforts to move parishes to-

ward a more communal model continued. Specifically, St. Michael's and a network of post-RENEW parishes asked me to help generate materials for parishes that were closing the fifth and last semester of RENEW. Along with the late Gorman Sullivan, O. Carm., noted initiation expert and liturgist Dawn Mayer Melendez, a long-time colleague and pastoral minister, Father Bill Moriarity, at the time pastor of St. John's in Streamwood, Sister Kathleen LaPlume, also of St. John's, I began a pastoral effort entitled Parish Spirituality. In Parish Spirituality we generated catechetical materials and also family, home-based material that facilitated people in the sharing of faith, sacred Scripture, and prayer. In generating materials for Parish Spirituality, I insisted we adhere to the principles of adult learning. Specifically, I insisted that no materials be produced until we did a systematic listening to the parishioners of the parishes involved in the project. Gorman Sullivan and I, from our background in the catechumenate, likewise encouraged that any future materials also be grounded in the Sunday liturgy, specifically in the readings from the lectionary. As the project unfolded in planning, booklets A, B, and C emerged for each of the six-week series of small group experiences. (There were six six-week gatherings altogether.) Booklet A was the adult catechetical resource, intended for use in the small groups. Booklet B was the resource for home use, specifically engaging parents and children in discussion on the same issues as those contained in Booklet A, but in home-oriented language. Booklet C contained scriptural reflections on the Sunday readings, as well as suggestions for art, environment, and bulletin covers. The idea behind booklets A, B, and C was somehow to provide the whole parish, whether in small groups using Booklet A or not, with a common experience.

After listening to parishioners in the twelve parishes networked in Parish Spirituality, we discerned and articulated the following areas of interest and concern: People wanted to know more about Jesus from a scriptural perspective; people wanted to know more about prayer and how to pray; there was also interest in the historical evolution of the sacraments; there was continuing interest from the RENEW years in principles of morality and social justice; a highly valued need (and the series that was most well received) was improving relationships, using gospel values; a final pragmatic area that we discussed was the many different kinds of small groups that could exist within a parish. The titles in sequence of production were:

- A Praying Community
- Jesus: Teacher, Savior, Healer, Lord
- Sacraments Alive
- Kingdom Response
- Improving Christian Relationships
- Parish: Community of Communities

These materials were produced for three years by the Office for Chicago Catholic Evangelization, which Dawn Melendez and I codirected. Of particular importance to me was the last booklet, intended to help parishes form small groups without someone always producing materials for them. I have been impressed by Bernard Lee and Michael Cowan's book on small communities, *Dangerous Memories*. In that work they isolate four core dynamics always involved in effective small groups: prayer, breaking open Scripture, sharing life, and service. I am convinced that if we could help people adopt an interior discipline around these values and behaviors, the nature of catechetical materials would cease to be a crucial issue. The interior discipline for small groups, as well as a snapshot of different ways people could be in a small group, was the focus of the last series of the three-year cycle. I am pleased to report that over half of the parishes involved in the Parish Spirituality project have gone on in the evolution of small groups, after Parish Spirituality ceased production as a series. Some of the parishes have retained Parish Spirituality as the name of other small group efforts.

In the summer of 1993 I moved to Holy Family in Inverness. In October 1992 I left the Office for Chicago Catholic Evangelization after thirteen years to accept a new position as coordinator of the former Mundelein Center of Religious Education at the Institute of Pastoral Studies at Loyola University in Chicago. I must say that the joint experience of coordinating a new center, teaching in the areas of evangelization and small communities, and also serving as the coordinator of the catechumenate and Evangelization, Stewardship and Training at Holy Family were a happy marriage. I feel I have had the best of two worlds—the intellectual stimulation of a university setting and the grassroots experience of parish life.

Holy Family began as a parish in 1984. The founding pastor Med Laz had the vision that he did not want just to develop another parish of programs and organizations. He very much wanted the parish to be rooted in small groups and community. The early years of the parish all took place in people's homes. But something happened as the parish moved out of its "childhood" years. There was a need to develop buildings, a church, meeting rooms where people could gather together with an identity as parish. The focus turned more and more to the building of structures. Through no one's fault the parish moved away from its small community emphasis. The parish is situated in a densely populated, rapidly growing suburb. The growth of the area somewhat depersonalized the parish. A parish of several hundred families quickly became several thousand. When I arrived at the parish, there was a felt need in the parish to return to its origin—its font. The parish council in 1992 established a core learning community that was commissioned to spend one year exploring models of small communities so that Holy Family could learn from a benchmarking process. In a parish reorganization effort, the position of coordinator of Evangelization, Stewardship, and Training developed. I assumed that role and began working with this existing core learning community.

In beginning work on small groups, we as a core group made it clear to the council and the staff that we did not see ourselves as agents of a new *program*. Rather we saw ourselves as facilitators of a paradigm shift for the parish.

The core community has learned some lessons in our time together. One of the most significant lessons shared has been the importance of patience in working a process within the parish toward the new paradigm. Small groups cannot just be "sprung" on a parish. The parish needs to be ministered to and educated as the new paradigm emerges. A congregation must first be helped to see and understand the need for small groups. In many "maintenance-oriented" parishes, things seem to be "going along fine." "Why tamper with success?" some might ask. Thus, it is of crucial importance for leaders in the paradigm shift process to demonstrate that the old paradigm is not working, or not working with as much success as it once did. Parishioners further need to see how small groups, or any new paradigm, embody the values and priorities that they cherish, that small groups are an expression of what they hold sacred. They also need to see that a new innovation in no way tramples upon or destroys any aspect of parish life that they deem important. Parishioners need to begin to see small groups as operating out of a vision of parish that is congruent with theirs. When people sense that a proposed new project is connected in vision and goals with what they believe about parish life; when they are helped to see one model of parish is not as effective as it once was and another model might accomplish the goals of parish life more successfully, they might begin to embrace the new innovation. If a leadership group skips this process and tries to push the paradigm shift without much grassroots consultation, the movement toward small communities will inevitably fail.

What has become obvious to me is the need for communication between and among all in the parish about the shift toward small groups. The conversation needs to happen with "opinion makers," those people in leadership positions in the parish, members of the parish council, people who have been in the community for a long time as well as newcomers. It is very important to be inclusive in the reeducation of the parish. The absence of such inclusiveness can sabotage the movement toward a new paradigm. A new paradigm needs the support and legitimacy that comes from opinion makers, and all parishioners are opinion makers.

At Holy Family, our core learning community worked toward the careful planning of a successful pilot of small groups. Specifically we decided on the model of small communities based on lectionary-oriented materials. Leading up to our kick-off date in Lent 1994, we have had several events that we used to communicate with and educate the congregation about the possibility of a new model of parish. In November 1993 we held an evening of renewal. People in ministry on a volunteer basis in the parish were invited to attend. We sent out over one thousand invitations, hoping for a substantial response. About 140 people attended. I personally was disappointed in the numbers, but I had to remind myself and the people I was working with that the movement toward a communal model of parish is countercultural. The church in the United States and Western Europe reflects the culture of individualism and independence around us. Thus the call to the communal will always be an approach/avoidance conflict. There will be some who will be drawn to the communal and others who will be opposed to such a church, parishioners like those that St. Paul spoke of, who want to "eat their own supper" at Eucharist. And so we joyfully embraced those who attended the renewal evening entitled "Back to the Future."

The title was chosen to suggest a number of things. What is the future church going to look like? In my presentation that night I spoke of the Acts 2 church—the church at its birth, which I described earlier in the book. I suggested that perhaps the Holy Spirit is pushing us back to the paradigm that we find at the origins of our church.

Father Med Laz, the pastor, tried to approach the theme of "Back to the Future" from a very parochial standpoint. In his presentation he said that Holy Family parish, indeed all parishes, began with a highly communal motif. But, he said, sometimes as a parish ages, some of that relational, communal motif is lost. In encouraging the parish to go back to the future, he was encouraging Holy Family to go back and retrieve some of what the parish was in danger of losing, namely its relational, interpersonal roots. The evening closed with several parishioners reflecting on how they had embraced change in their lives, how it was difficult to change, but in hindsight, that change was very fruitful. This was included to highlight the similarities in the struggle in both personal and corporate change.

The closing ritual was a movement of platters of baked bread from the altar at the center of the church to smaller tables scattered throughout the church. People who attended were encouraged to go around the small tables, break the bread, and to give it to another person and say to that person, "We Are Bread for Each Other." The other person took and ate the bread. We hoped to give people a feeling of how, in small groups, people actually become bread for one another.

I thought that the evening of renewal was too long, too wordy and verbal. I do think, however, we gave those in attendance an intuitive feel for what small communities were all about. In December 1993, we followed up with an evening on "A Taste of Small Communities." We invited all who attended the first night of renewal to come back and experience what an actual evening might feel or look like during Lent. Some sixty people attended. Those who attended reported a very positive experience of being in a small group. People were asked to submit their names if they were interested in becoming leaders, if and when these small communities came into being. I believe with that night and with the ongoing conversation within the parish, contagion and passion for small groups had begun. It was from the people who attended the two renewal evenings that we largely found our small group leaders.

There had to be some other movements during the gestation period of moving toward the launching of a successful pilot. Obviously the people who were proponents of the vision of a more communal parish possessed a vision of what small groups could be. That wisdom could not be overlooked. Rather, it had to be and still must be shared in an ongoing way. Reports from the core learning committee had to be given to the parish staff, the parish council, and the extended staff. We constantly had to speak of the vision and engage in ongoing education of leadership people as well as the congregation as a whole. We communicated with the congregation through mailings, pulpit announcements, and bulletin announcements. Finally, as Lent 1994 approached,

I preached at all the Masses in January about the importance of small groups, and Lent as a time to experience conversion.

We called one small group project "Crossroads." The ministry has continued to bear that name. That weekend we had sign-up Sunday. We had multiple opportunities for sign-up: on cards in the pews, in the narthex of the church, or via mail. Over 750 people out of 2,800 registered households said they wanted to be in small groups. Part of our strategies in soliciting people for small groups was to write to people in charge of ministry groups, inviting them to re-imagine themselves not just as a task group but as a small Christian community. We tried to tap into the natural weaving or webbing that might call people together, like a common ministry. That was also very effective in soliciting people for the movement. Marketing experts have told me that the huge jump in numbers of those interested largely came from a rather passionate witness that I gave in preaching on the weekend. Because one of staff was speaking on small groups people sensed that this was a staff endorsement of the project.

As the time got nearer, it was necessary to train group leaders. They were trained in two evening sessions and a Saturday session for those who could not attend evenings. The essence of the training consisted of these key elements: an overview of the history of small groups in the Catholic Christian experience; the project in the parish and the various roles needed to make the project happen; and above all, the importance of the role of small group leaders. It was emphasized in training that the key roles of a small group leader were to create a safe environment for people to meet in, to grow in human-relations skills, and to grow in the ability to do theological reflection and faith sharing. We simplified theological reflection and described it as helping people connect ordinary human experience with Scripture and our faith tradition.

We created roles that were assumed by members of our core learning community, the roles of the coaches or mentors as they are called now. The mentor is not to be a group leader but nonetheless needs to be trained in the skills of group leadership. The mentor serves as a middle manager. Each mentor has five or six small groups that he or she ministers to. It is their job to meet with the group leaders on a regular basis, attend their meetings at least once, and during a season of meetings to troubleshoot and to report back to the staff coordinator. The role of the mentor is largely to connect staff, coordinator, the core group, and group leaders and to assure quality control in the groups assigned to him or her. If there are any problems it is the role of the mentor "to mend the hole" in the group. Dr. Paul Cho and John Hurston teach that if there is a problem in a small group, there is a hole in the evangelical net, the net being a metaphor for catching people via the evangelizing that takes place in small groups. A good net is made up of horizontal relationships of people in a group that interconnect with vertical relationships of authority, wisdom, and coordination. A good net is an intersecting of those kinds of relationships. If there is a hole in the net, the mending must take place as easily and quickly as possible.

The group training that I mentioned is certainly not representative of training in its entirety. Training will take place on a regular basis as our small groups continue to develop. After Lent we evaluated the initial small group experience to affirm what was good in it and to reshape it where that was needed. We decided to maintain our lectionary-based groups in subsequent fall and Lenten periods for those who wished to be in such groups, but also to expand to a track two which would be based on discerned needs. Our initial

track two was going to be a series on relationships, based
on one of the old Parish Spirituality series. Other options
might include family groups, which gather clusters of families for family-based religious education. This was coordinated collaboratively with our child-formation division.
However we planned to expand, we wanted to make sure
that it was around needs and that we had the resources to
deliver on what we had promised. Other interesting suggestions that arose for expansion of the Crossroads innovation
were as follows: High School Youth Ministry was re-imagined
as a network of small intergenerational groups that met at
least twice a month in adult mentors' homes; the women's
ministry program volunteered to provide input in devising
group materials the next year, so that specific women's issues
might make their way into some editions of the common
catechetical materials. A mothers' group asked for similar
consideration, so that Crossroads groups might better adress
young mothers' experiences. The child formation division
requested a satellite process for catechists during the "off
seasons" from catechizing, to engage catechetical ministries
in faith formation. Wonderful suggestions were made regarding the ongoing training and formation of small group leaders. The group leaders themselves requested formation at
least every eight weeks. It was hoped that "small group leaders" would emerge as a free-standing ministry, with official
commissionings happening at weekend liturgies. Some of
the topics discerned for immediate ongoing trainings were:

- the importance of prayer and ritual in the small group
  meeting;

- the future direction of church;

- the group leader as pastor;

- fish-bowl experience on leading small group skills;

- open forum on typical problems in directing small groups.

In addition to all these directions that emerged in evaluation, it was proposed that another constant in small group ministry be the formation of some of the core learning group who would always be ready to launch new people in new groups. This would require a kind of ad hoc immediacy in training small group leaders. The core learning group discerned Lyman Coleman's *All Aboard* series as a good primer for engaging in this ministry of starting groups.

If we discovered anything from this experience, it was perhaps that we moved too fast. We had more people sign up for small groups than we had group leaders. We used last-minute efforts to go after small group leaders and train them so that small groups could be launched.

In this chapter, I have been sharing how one parish undertook the most significant pastoral steps that I ever experienced toward a new paradigm. It was important to do much group processing throughout the parish in preparation for the pilot. The pilot needed to be carefully planned and launched. The pilot needed to be successful! The materials that we used for Crossroads were easily adaptable by the group leader if he or she desired to move the discussion in other directions. However, we did not ever want to lose the core movements of

- looking at the past week; to discern how God had spoken in the ordinary events of life

- sharing the lectionary readings and faith-sharing questions

- looking at the rest of the week, to discuss how to put the gospel into practice.

If the steps that we followed at Holy Family in the process of moving to a new paradigm are followed in other parishes, I believe there can be success. With a successful pilot accomplished, people will also be willing to go a step further in future endeavors to maximize and expand innovation and paradigm shift.

6

The Communal Parish

*I*n addition to working in a parish as an associate pastor and the coordinator of Evangelization, Stewardship, and Training, I have also, as mentioned earlier, served as the coordinator of the Center for Evangelization, Catechesis, and Religious Education at Loyola University, and for many years have been the president of the National Center for Evangelization and Parish Renewal. These two latter positions have enabled me, these last few years, not only to work in the parish to which I am assigned, but have also given me the opportunity to travel. As I serve and consult in evangelization and new paradigms of parish, I have learned a great deal as I have attempted to teach others.

Currently I direct a project entitled "The Communal Parish" out of the National Center for Evangelization and Parish Renewal. Besides Holy Family parish, there are seven other parishes contractually engaged in this project. It is our hope that as we grow as a consultation service, more and more parishes will become part of the Communal Parish Project and gradually become a pastoral alliance for excellence in parish renewal. The Communal Parish Project operates on the basis of yearly contracts. Parishes can contract for one, two, or three years of the project. While we are operating on the basis of yearly contracts, we know that the work for each year may indeed expand the parameter of one year; and so, various individuals and groups of people may be fine-tuning, continuing to work on one level of the project, while others perhaps will be beginning a new era or new level of the project.

The Communal Parish Project—Year One

The first movement or year one of the Communal Parish Project is titled "Getting Started in Small Groups and Theological Reflection." The first step that parishes in this project need to take is establishing a core learning community, similar to the one at Holy Family, that will take some time with us as consultants and with their parish staff to study and pray about a new paradigm for parish life, namely the communal. In fact, before a parish staff buys into the Communal Parish Project, there needs to be a commitment by all the staff members that they indeed feel that small groups and small communities are the model of church to which the Holy Spirit is calling us. Any one of us as individuals can start a small group in our living room and meet weekly; but if we are about the work of parish revivification, or to use the stronger term of Gerald Arbuckle, "re-founding," then the parish staff and leadership must be on board and moving in the same direction for this refounding to take place. As the core community does its work of study, reading, and consultation experiences, ongoing efforts are engaged in by the communal parish team and others in the project to educate the congregation as a whole, as well as organizations and communities that are already existing, about the intuitive sense that leadership in the various parts of the world have, that God seems to be calling us to greater, more intense experiences of community.

Of the seven parishes enrolled in the Communal Parish project, six of them started their activities around the same time as Holy Family. Therefore there has been the advantage of interfeeding between and among the parishes involved. The sequence of events has been very much congruent with the flow of events in the development of small groups at Holy Family. In these other parishes, there has been ongoing mass education about the new model of parish. The various parishes have also engaged in subscription Sundays, providing multiple opportunities for people to participate in small communities at various times with various kinds of people. There also has been in the other parishes the solicitation of small group leaders. As at Holy Family parish, a crucial step has been small group facilitator training, and within that the explanation of the overall plan, vision, or system by which small groups will develop. Therefore in each parish in which we have conducted training, we have called for the creation of the following roles:

- the staff coordinator or consultant who will be ultimately responsible for starting and networking small groups;

- the administrative assistant who assists the coordinator in the myriad details involved in a project like this;

- the person or people who will assist with marketing small groups to those who attend church as well as those who do not;

- the quality-control people—namely the role of the coach or mentor—the middle-management person who will oversee five or six groups and resource and minister to them. As Dr. Paul Cho and John Hurston have taught, the coaches (they refer to them as district leaders or section leaders) are the quality contact people that the staff coordinator can connect with great immediacy to ensure the quality of small group life.

- the small group leader, who creates an environment of comfort and hospitality, is equipped with human-relations skills and the skills needed to connect sacred Scripture with experience. This latter set of skills is what is called theological reflection, or as we refer to it in working with ordinary folks, the skills of faith-sharing.

In terms of membership in the group, the project team is teaching the parishes and group leaders involved that membership comes from two directions. One is a subscription weekend. After a process of education in the parish, a subscription weekend does bring to the surface people who want to belong to groups. In addition, group leaders and members also have the responsibility to connect with people who might profit from small group experiences and invite them in. Two things should be added at this point: the addition of new members always involves the process of dialogue, contracting, and recontracting within the group. No one member can decide to bring another person into the group without the whole group being involved in the process of deciding and discerning. Lyman Coleman has a discipline that he encourages small groups to engage in so they do not fall into becoming cliques or enclaves. He encourages small groups always to have a vacant chair present at every meeting to serve as a reminder to all that there is someone out there who could benefit from being a part of a small group, and who also in turn would enrich and nurture the life of the small group.

In training leaders for small group facilitation, one of the basic skills the Communal Parish Project has had to engage in is how to use the materials prepared for faith-sharing and theological reflection. We are in the process of creating our own lectionary-based materials, similar to those used at Holy Family. The other parishes, however, reshaped the materials to fit the needs of the parishes involved. Many of the parishes involved had different demographics, and they had concerns that were somewhat different from those of Holy Family. The methodology of each session, however, has remained basically the same for all the parishes involved. The group leader calls those in attendance to prayer; there is then a review of the week or a sharing of what has happened to each member since the last meeting. The second part of the review is the discernment of God's revelation as it is present in the stories that have been told. The specific question asked is, "Did anyone hear God speaking in the stories we shared with each other?" Then there is a proclamation of Scripture, one or more of the readings from the following week's liturgy, a review of a short exegetical and hermeneutical reflection on a given passage, and then the faith-sharing questions. These questions are open-ended, intended to solicit storytelling rather than information sharing. It is hoped that in the storytelling there is also the sharing of faith experiences, wisdom, of how God and church are having an impact on people's lives.

The project leaders hope that people leave with a collective wisdom that was not there before the group meeting. The faith-sharing around the Scripture segment is followed by a looking to the rest of the week component in which people ask the question, "What can I concretely do to live the message of the Scripture these next seven days?" We encourage participants to be concrete and behavioral. Five of the seven parishes working in tandem with Holy Family are also asking another question: "What could *we* as a group do to put the gospel into action?" These parishes are very much trying to shake parishioners out of isolation and independence into healthy interdependence and cooperation around the issues of social justice. All of this is followed by a closing prayer that is done facing the doors and windows, a circle facing outward in an attempt to give participants a feeling for outreach and mission.

There has been some discussion about where to place a break in the course of the two-hour meeting. Some groups are placing it right after the Scripture sharing. Other groups, especially those made up of people who have been in small groups before, say that refreshments ought to be nearby throughout the meeting, but there should be a full meeting that takes in all the parts of a given session and then ten to fifteen minutes ought to be saved at the bottom end of the meeting for fellowship and refreshments.

So the use of materials is a big part of the training for the parishes involved in the project. Giving people basic skills for theological reflection is also an important part of training. Some of the components of theological reflection that we would stress in our training programs are as follows:

- Be sensitive to human experience, realize that God speaks through human experience.

- As your group unfolds, encourage people to bring their stories to group meetings, especially for the first part of the meeting.

- Learn to listen to human experience and be discerning.

Group leaders are taught to listen to the voice of God that is quietly and subtly being spoken in human experience.

Group leaders are encouraged to realize how important the news is and how important the culture is. What is going on in the world, the neighborhood? What are the dominant values or attitudes coming at us almost by osmosis from the

culture? Can we name some of those attitudes, can we discern, articulate which of those dominant images are of God
and which are contrary to the gospel?

It is important to train group leaders to listen to Scripture—but not in a fundamentalist sense. As in the Little
Rock Scripture Study sessions, small group leaders should
be given some insight into what exegesis is, or that movement backward to discover the meaning and intent of the
Scripture's author. And group leaders should also be given
hermeneutical skills—the skill of moving forward to the
present moment to discern how a given Scripture passage
speak to us today.

I think that it is very important to sensitize group leaders,
in the process of theological reflection, to the importance of
tradition. I am not speaking of the trappings of traditional-
ism. I was at a meeting recently where a young, born-again
fundamentalist had an immediate, negative reaction to the
word *tradition*. I had to take some time to convince this
young man that tradition is not the negative thing that he
had come to think it is in his born-again experience. When
I speak of "tradition" I am speaking of the core tenets of our
faith as they have been handed down to us over the centuries.
When I speak of tradition I am speaking of the Nicene
Creed, the Apostles' Creed, the credal statements of We
believe in God, We believe in Jesus, We believe in redemption, We believe in the Resurrection, We believe in the sacramental life, We believe in the mystery of the church, We
believe in eternal life, We believe in the second coming of
Christ. Those statements sound perhaps somewhat arid, but
they are in fact like eggs to be broken open. Credal talk is
symbol talk that reflects a great deal of religious experience.
The goal in a small group session is to connect tradition,
culture, and personal stories as well as Scripture sharing,

all pushing toward the net result of hearing the voice of God in the present moment—revelation.

In doing theological reflection the small group leader, with the support of catechetical materials, is trying to do just that. He or she encourages the small group to listen to their experiences, the news, the culture, Scripture, tradition, and then pose the question "What is God saying?" Other questions follow in theological reflection like "What will my position be now that I have connected these pieces of being Christian in the context of a small group? Will it be different than it was before the meeting began?" Then comes the critical question that Tom Groome always poses in his shared praxis: "Based on our sharing, now what should we do?" This action-orientation is the reason that we have included "Looking at the Rest of the Week" in our materials. It is to move people from "head faith" into faith that takes action—whether it is personal or communal action.

Besides theological-reflection skills the project team continues to train people in human-relations skills and discussion skills. Imparting these human-relations skills involves some time given to input, but a great deal of time needs to be given to *practicing* these skills. The skills that we highlight are accurate listening, how to help open people up through door-opener comments, acknowledgment responses that draw people out of themselves, listening checks in which the group leader is given the skill to check out with the speaker the accuracy with which he or she has listened. Connected to active or accurate listening, restatement or paraphrasing skills are presented that basically show a person who has spoken that he or she has been heard. The skills of summarizing the conversation that has been shared so far in the group is shared and practiced. So also is the skill of being able to notice nonverbal clues. The skills of listening for and responding to feelings and using open-

ended questions that permit storytelling and specific questions that elicit information are also practiced. It is very
important to give group leaders ample time to appropriate
these skills in action and not just give the skills verbally in
an instructional fashion.

At a recent Communal Parish project training session over
the course of a morning, leaders sat in artificial groups made
up of colleague coleaders. Each of the leaders had to take
part of the meeting and act as a leader. In turn, colleague-
leaders took time after each segment to critique and offer
suggestions to the person who served as a leader in the
last segment.

Also part of the initial training of leaders for this first year
of trying to initiate small Christian communities is what we
call *discerning roles in a group.* In addition to the leader in
an individual group, there should also be an assistant leader.
There could also be a phone-call minister who calls people
to remind them of the upcoming meeting. There could or
should be a prayer leader. There may be some who would
be willing to devise a family component and take children
who may attend the small group meeting on occasion to
different parts of the home for sharing, and then bring them
together with parents for a family ritual or sharing. There
is the ministry of host or hostess. We suggest that the ministry of hospitality be shared equally with all the members of
the group. All members of the group should see themselves
as evangelizers; all are called to reach out and invite new
members in, based on the group's evolving contract. Above
all in this section of training, we are trying to avoid a nouveau
clericalism, or the group leaders taking on responsibility for
all the ministry and needs present in the small group. The
Communal Parish project suggests that initial small group
meetings are of a short-term commitment nature. The small
groups will meet during the fall and Lent. As with the Holy

Family groups, any groups that discern or decide that they want more meetings are more than free to recontract with each other for those meetings. It was the wisdom of the Communal Parish project team that for the sake of stability it would be good to stay in one home or meeting for the entire semester or season of meetings.

The initial training for Lent groups in 1993–1994 was followed up by a debriefing meeting held during Lent, midway in the initial pilot, for all who were small group leaders. This Saturday morning experience was an opportunity for everyone involved to get together to share stories, experiences, and role-play around problem situations they might have experienced in their groups. This was followed by the evaluation meeting after Lent to look at all aspects of the first wave of small group gatherings. What was studied were the materials. Were they helpful in leading groups to faith-sharing? Also evaluated was the style of training and the communication patterns that existed between mentors and group leaders and the staff coordinators. The evaluations were also used to reshape the process for future small group trainings and gatherings. As of the writing of this book, plans were being made for the fall 1994 sessions to be held in these seven parishes.

A few directions were discerned for the future. Some people who had been involved in the process suggested that there be materials developed for family-based groups and clusters of families meeting together. Several of the parishes are going to follow Holy Family's lead in having a track two during the fall on improving relationships. There also was a convergence of opinion that small group leadership needs to become a free-standing ministry in the parishes with training and formation occuring at a minimum of every eight weeks. Small group leaders ought not to meet just in close proximity to a season of small group meetings, but rather the year round.

The Communal Parish Project—Year Two

Reanimating Religious Education

Parishes choosing to continue in the project's second year will be helped to analyze the status quo in religious education and sacramental catechesis, and then re-imagine these ministries for the future. While each parish in the project will undoubtedly create unique models that reflect the people and culture of the parishes, we the consulting team hold to certain heart-values:

- the religious education of children needs to break out of the classroom-schooling model and explore alternative models;

- those alternative models ought to be family-based: either a catechetical ministry to a cluster of families, or the parents in a cluster of families being enabled to alternate in the role of catechist to the rest of the adults and children;

- the nature of future alternative models ought to involve a marriage of lectionary-based catechesis, which roots each family in the centrality of the Word of God and the Eucharist, with systematic catechesis (in a nonschooling way) joined to the lectionary emphasis.* Systematic

---

*James Dunning and others prefer the notion of "liturgy of the word" catechesis, which suggests a commitment to contextualize all catechesis in Scripture and liturgy, without being wedded to a given Sunday's readings.

catechesis is the gradual immersion of children and families into community (the large assembly, the cluster of families, the domestic church of home). It is through interaction with the community, through liturgy, teachingmoments, opportunities for service, and the social life of the community that God's Word and the tradition are assimilated;

- the faith transmitted in catechetical efforts must be simultaneously informational, formational, and transformational, arising from but also contributing to community;

- all child-family focus efforts should be complemented by groups and ministries that foster home-church, namely events that contribute toward skill-building in marriage, parenting, reconstituted families, and any other issues related to the enrichment of the household;

- these catechetical efforts should include programs that are needs-based adult religious education helping adults to connect the issues of everyday life and reality with the gospel and/or faith tradition;

- there needs to be a visionary who serves as coordinator or director or animator of all catechetical ministries, uniting often disparate efforts in a seamless fabric of vision and strategy for religious education;

- the natural rhythm of the liturgical year and the steps of the Order of Initiation are the process by which catechetical efforts ought to proceed.

The Communal Parish project invites parishes to re-imagine religious-education efforts around the paradigms of household and groups of households (families). Though texts and series that are friendly to these core values are important, of greater importance is the practice or discipline of gathering families. As mentioned earlier, the educational system can train catechists to work with clusters of families, or train parents to alternate in the role of catechist in their various family clusters.

In a parish moving from the schooling model, it might be strategically effective to ask highly motivated or interested parents to participate in pilot projects, one with the catechist serving a cluster of families, the other with parents taking greater responsibility for catechizing their children. With two pilots, process coordinators will have a better sense of problem areas or areas of concern as they try to expand the models to the rest of the families involved in the religious-education process.

Some issues that need to be addressed in moving toward a communal mode of religious education include the following: How should families use their time together? Should there be separate times for adult catechesis for the parents and also time for children's catechesis? Should the bulk of time be in a group of the whole, using a catechetical methodology like Thomas Groome's *Shared Praxis?* Another possibility could be to build into the methodology large group experiences that engage all the families in a cluster, but also some individual family time for households to engage intramurally. It should be noted that, as we talk of family, in an average parish over 50 percent will not be of the once typical two parents present in the home, the parents in their first and only marriage type. Instead, many households will be made up of single-parent situations, blended family situations, or situations in which someone other than blood parents serve as the children's guardians. The role of ritual, or the significance of liturgical catechesis, should also be discussed and planned for. Rituals have the power to bring the essence of what is being taught into the hearts of the participants. Ritual impacts the imagination, which is the deposit of the primary, dominant images that motivate us. The Order of Initiation, in fact, has taught us that effective religious education occurs when evangelization and catechesis are joined to ritual and pastoral care all in the context of community. Consideration should also be given to activities that families can engage in together in the home, to foster spiritual growth in between these sessions.

The major pieces of this renewed religious education ecology are:

- regular, consistent offerings of children's liturgy of the Word, offered at several Masses each weekend, with a coordinator of this effort engaged to insure that these experiences are qualitative;

- multilevel family-based religious education tracks with various coordinators (e.g., preschool, primary, intermediate, junior high);

- home-church ministries, which provide both children and adults with theory and skills in relationship-building; a coordinator is needed here too; in the project we call this position the home-church consultant; others may refer to it as the family life minister;

- an adult religious education component, facilitated by a coordinator, which offers regular large group, needs-based experiences, respecting the principles of adult learning;

- a director/animator of the entire effort.

One of the parishes in the project posed a dilemma that we will deal with in more depth later in the book. It is the issue of parallel development. One catechetical coordinator, at a recent meeting, asked how she could practically move

toward a new paradigm with such a large clientele still wedded to the schooling model. I answered that for a while we
may have parallel processes in catechetics in the parishes
involved. It may be necessary to offer a level one of the
"tried and true," while in an ever-expanding way offering
opportunities for the family-based, communal style for those
who wish to be a part of that. Such a gradual emergence of
a new paradigm might better respect parishioners' need for
time to appropriate change, as well as the catechetical coordinator's need for time to reshape operations effectively. As
mentioned earlier, operating on a "pilot" basis also allows
room for mistakes and evaluations, learning and reshaping
of the project.

While still in the area of religious education, let us raise
another issue—that of collaboration leading to consistent vision and strategies for religious education. One of the primary roles of a director/coordinator/animator of catechetical
ministries is to call the various coordinators together not
only on the level of vision but also on the level of strategy.
A perfect arena in which to model and demonstrate collaboration in vision and strategy is calendaring. In the compartmentalization model of parish life, each parish program or
division does its own calendaring, irrespective of the operations of other ministries. Often parish bulletins reflect this:
a flurry of wonderful things happening in a scattershot sort
of way. The overall director of this division might challenge
coordinators to create a wholistic calendar in which adults,
children, families, and the home-church experience qualitative moments of growth that are held in such a way as not
to compete with other qualitative events in the parish. In
turn, on another level of staff, the director of catechetical
ministries ought to collaborate with his or her counterparts
in liturgy, pastoral care, youth ministry, and any other parish
divisions to present to the entire parish a wholistic calendar
that reflects parish-wide collaboration in vision and strategy.

The skeleton of the calendar should always be the liturgical year and the journey of catechumens, candidates, and all of us toward Easter and renewal in the paschal mystery.

A question that may be emerging in the minds of attentive readers is: The author has not even gotten to sacramental catechesis and he already has adults in two kinds of groups: self-nurture, adult-focused groups, and groups for family religious education. Now we are turning to sacramental catechesis. How many groups can one person belong to? If you have several children, to which groups do you go?

The only answer I can give is that paradigm shift is messy and nonprogrammatic. If an adult feels called to several group experiences simultaneously, he or she will have to operate on the principles of common sense, what is possible and what is best for one's children, and what is spiritually self-nurturing. This may result in a tapestry of various communal experiences sewn together in faith and good will. Parish staff and others ought to help in a discernment process that facilitates such experiences. In no way should there be a "police-state mentality" that legalizes this communal approach. That would seriously impede what the new paradigm is attempting to accomplish. On the ideal level, however, as the paradigm emerges it would be my hope that most of the needs of a typical parishioner, family, or household would be met in one single group. Membership in such a group by individuals or as family ideally would address many pastoral needs—religious education, spiritual direction, pastoral care, youth ministry, and others. We will return to this issue when we consider the third segment of the Communal Parish project.

Reanimating Sacramental Catechesis

I believe we have the best potential to evangelize nominal members through preparation for sacramental moments, or sacramental catechesis. Here also the small group can be used as the vehicle, the medium through which to do this ministry. Too often, sacramental catechesis is a largely cerebral experience, often preparing children for the reception of a holy thing or to celebrate a holy event. Sacramental catechesis, wrote James LoPresti some years ago, should always be preparation for a way of life. If that ecclesiological view is true, then it follows that the Christian way of life is communal, and preparation ought to be in the context of the communal. A word of caution at this juncture, however. Sacramental preparation is notorious for its legalization—if someone does not attend "x" amount of meetings, he or she, or their child, will not get their holy thing. In re-imagining this ministry toward a more communal modality, we must ensure quality preparation while also facilitating a much more life-giving, nourishing environment than this ministry has experienced before—community.

The parishes that make up the project currently have various staff members serving as coordinators of preparation for sacraments. In one parish, the associate pastor coordinates Baptismal and Marriage preparation. One of the catechetical coordinators cares for Reconciliation and First Eucharist preparation. The youth minister coordinates Confirmation preparation. I am sure that such a division of labor exists in many parishes. Another model could be to have a central director, coordinator, or animator to consult the various coordinators of sacraments. If this latter model is not feasible, it is nonetheless vital that the various sacramental coordinators synergize toward a common vision and common strategies for sacramental catechesis.

In the project, we are encouraging two heart-disciplines:

(1) that sacramental preparation be done in small groups, or in clusters of families where children are involved;

(2) and that the journey toward the sacramental moment be modeled on the Order of Christian Initiation.

Years ago Tad Guzie suggested these disciplines in *The Book of Sacramental Basics*. He encouraged that for each sacrament there be a process:

- of general inquiry or evangelization ----->

- followed by a public ritual of beginning the journey toward the sacramental celebration ----->

- and a period of suitable formation ----->

- leading to a public ritual of beginning proximate preparation ----->

- resulting in an integral celebration of the sacrament ----->

- and the individual or family finding a new place with God and the community.

The various ministries in need of coordination in this subset are as follows:

- the Order of Christian Initiation and the Order of Initiation for Children

- Baptism

- Confirmation

- First Eucharist

- First Reconciliation and Reconciliation processes for inactives (Returning Catholics)

- Marriage

- Anointing of the Sick (Liturgical theologian Regis Duffy believes there is a catechumenal dimension even with this sacrament. He contends that the sacramental minister is not just bringing the comfort of the community to the person sidelined by sickness. The sacrament is also soliciting commitment and recommitment. Can the broken revow to the meaning of his or her baptism despite affliction or sickness?)

In both the religious education and sacramental subdivisions of the Communal Parish project, we are advocating the same kind of ministerial roles as those found in the first year of launching small groups:

- professional staff people serve as consultants, animators, and trainers;

- some parishioners invested in the processes are trained as coaches, the quality-control persons, who work intensively with five or six group leaders;

- group leaders in the religious education and sacramental components will most likely be trained catechists;

- the target population in religious education/sacramental efforts are never individuals, but rather individuals and their social context, that is, their families, households, or primary relationships.

The same kinds of concerns surface as we discuss sacramental catechesis and the sheer number of group meetings a parent especially might feel compelled to attend. As we do church "in between times," that is, in between paradigms, the principles of common sense, the spiritual well-being of children and the household, and the faith nurturance of the adults involved are all values to be kept in balance. I again speculate that as the new paradigm emerges, much of the ministry done in disparate groups will be done within one natural, organic group.

Phase Three—Two Churches in One Parish, Parallel Development Toward the New Paradigm

A colleague of mine, Presbyterian minister John de Beers, serving as a consultant to the Communal Parish project, used the phrase *parallel development* to aptly describe the scene a parish might find itself in after working on two levels of refounding according to a communal model. Simply put, this kind of movement will create two kinds of parishes existing in parallel fashion. There will be the parish of programs and organization, harnessed by a governance body, usually called the parish council. Such a parish might look like Diagram 1 (see p. 90) if it is organized well.

Though the terminology may change, I believe something equivalent to this model to be the most effective in harnessing volunteer ministries and volunteers in organizations in the 1970s–1980s program-organization parish. Staff and council's joint mission was and is to organize the activities of the parish, with the ministries and activities in turn having influence on the direction of the council, in fact often deciding, electing, or discerning who should be on the council. Within each of the ministerial or organizational divisions there would be micromanagement and organization going on to achieve effectiveness and efficiency in each unit.

Parallel to the above structures would be the Communal Parish. The evolving structure might look something like that which appears in Diagram 2 (see p. 92).

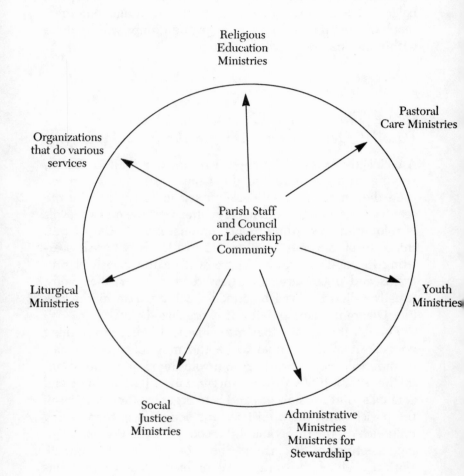

DIAGRAM 1

Diagram 2 attempts to visualize people in three strata of small group formation, using the common animation discipline of staff consulting/training: middle management, quality-control mentoring, and small group leaders.

The existential fact is that two different kinds of parishes are coexisting at this stage of the project. What do we do with the program-organization parish? Some would suggest the following: tell the people a new kind of parish is being born, and that the staff does not have the time to resource both; one has to die and another rise, so get on board. I find that approach abrasive and in the long run nonproductive. I would instead utilize the "convincing folks of a need" process, described in the chapter on Holy Family's move toward a new paradigm, that is, to talk to opinion makers, work toward a conversion of vision and goals, prepare successful pilots of communal experiences within each ministry division, and have successful launchings of them that, by entropy and contagion, will enhance the innovation. As I mentioned earlier, one "in-between-the-times" step may be to envision every ministry having two levels operative for a while: the traditional program-organizational-volunteer models with level two models of the communal also being tried.

As I study Catholic, mainline Protestant, and evangelical models of congregations moving toward the communal, I have come to have a more realistic outlook about paradigm shift. Perhaps parish organizations, volunteer ministries, and programs targeting articulated needs will be pieces of parish life that will be constant, that is, to some degree always in place. Along with Sabbath worship, they serve as a kind of ongoing posture of year-round reach-out and evangelization for entry-level parishioners or those desiring the basic services of a faith community. But we need to encourage parishioners to see beyond to God's dream, as revealed in Scripture and through Jesus: the communal, the more

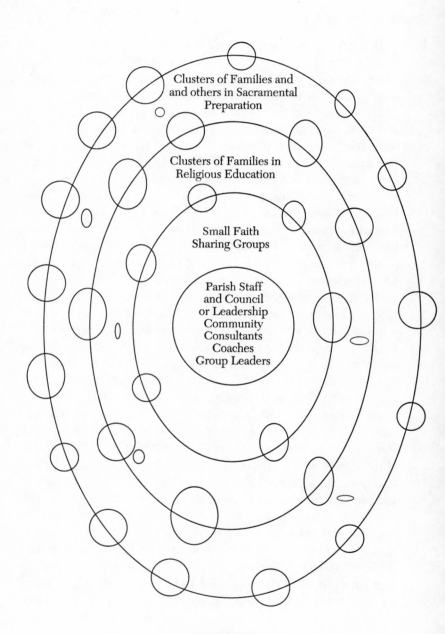

Clusters of Families and
and others in Sacramental
Preparation

Clusters of Families in
Religious Education

Small Faith
Sharing Groups

Parish Staff
and Council
or Leadership
Community
Consultants
Coaches
Group Leaders

DIAGRAM 2

highly relational parish. Thus, what we now know as basic parish operations would, in the future, always be experienced as a kind of threshold to something more. Parish life could be re-imagined to look something like Diagram 3.

Resembling Don Kimball's famous "wedge theory" of youth ministry, this vision realistically accepts that not every parishioner is going to see the need or want or accept more highly relational styles of parish life. Neither will some want to invest the commitment energy or exercise the responsibility that is needed for such a model.

A practical question that emerges from this discussion is, what will parish governance look like in the Communal Parish at the stage of parallel development? To the degree the parish is moving toward the communal model, its governance structure needs to mirror that. Rather than being the organism that harnasses volunteer ministries, programs, and organizations, the parish council instead would become the organizing force of communities. In such a model, the various groups and communities somehow discern how they are to be represented in the parish leadership community who, with the pastoral staff, do long-range planning, shaping, and evaluation of parish life. In some dioceses implementing the vision and strategies of the Movement for a Better World, there are regular gatherings of a parish assembly besides councils that reflect the communal mode. At these gatherings, the small communities that have been sectioned or zoned together, for efficient communication and also pastoral management, all meet together. The pastoral assembly provides an even more expansive form for communication, consensus governance, pastoral model innovation, and idea-swapping for small group life. It is crucial that small groups and communities gradually make their presence felt in parish governance structures, in terms of representation. A visualization of this can be found in Diagram 4 (see p. 96).

STATUS QUO OF PARISH LIFE

Weekend Worship

Volunteer Ministries

Programs Addressing
Needs

Organizations

Parish in ongoing
service and reach-out
via organizations
and ministries

**SMALL GROUPS
BECOMING COMMUNITIES**

Family/Cluster of
Families in Religious
Education

Small Group/
Family Sacramental
Catechesis

**SMALL CHRISTIAN
COMMUNITIES**

meet basic
ministerial and
faith-nurturance
needs and provide
opportunities
to serve in ongoing
relationships

DIAGRAM 3

If they do not, the vision and strategies of small groups may rest too much on the personality of an individual or the vision of one or more staff members. If and when they move out, there is the danger of the communal mode going with them. This vision and strategy interruption is a source of great pain and frustration in the lives of parishioners, who are at the mercy of diocesan personnel or placement boards. Parish councils need to become guarantors of a vision and strategy for parish life. Transitional professionals have no right to abort such long-term pastoral efforts. The biggest pastoral dilemma regarding small groups is not getting them started, but rather their ongoing continuation and support.

If I am correct in saying the programmatic side of the parish may always be with us, not as a permanent maintenance posture but rather re-imagined as an evangelization entrée to a more communal parish, then governance must reflect that reality. The parish leadership community (my preference to parish council) would become, in such cases, the coordinating organism of the parish in parallel development (see Diagram 4, p. 96).

Using again the dynamics of discernment over election, ministries and organizations as well as small groups would delegate representatives to serve in leadership positions.

We have discussed three possible levels of movement toward a paradigm shift: starting small groups, reanimating religious education and sacramental catechesis around communal and familial experiences, managing a parish "in between times," in parallel development. The delicate balance for pastoral leaders at this point in history is to have to maintain some semblance of the old model while experimenting with new forms. I cannot stress enough two principles for this situation:

(1) the importance of *benchmarking*, that is, studying others' models especially in the area of religious education

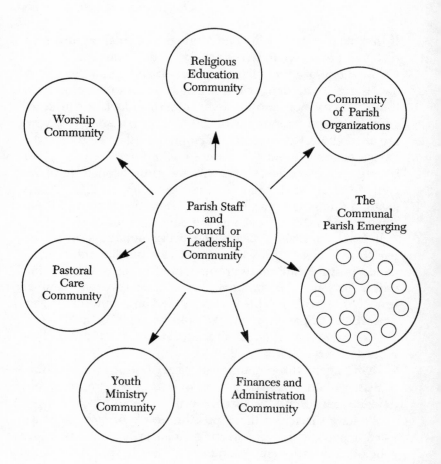

DIAGRAM 4

and sacramental catechesis and *launching pilots* of communal/family-based efforts; successful pilots, through contagion, breed enhancement of innovation;

(2) the importance of staffs and pastoral leaders creating a calendar together, respecting the movement of the liturgical year and the catechumenate, and inclusive of level one (old paradigm) and level two (the communal paradigm) offerings. The medium is the message: If leadership is experienced as collaborative and united in vision and strategy, that will hopefully gradually have an effect on the minds and hearts of parishioners in general, advancing the paradigm shift.

7

Ministry to Conversion Readiness

*A*s I reflect on the turning points or conversion experiences of my life, several constants from the rather diverse experiences emerge: most of the experiences that led to conversion were not planned for; most of the experiences involved a voiding out, an experience of pain or woundedness, or a breakdown; in all of these transforming experiences there were present to me people of faith who helped me find meaning, hope, and new life in apparent nonsense, confusion, or suffering. It is the last item that I would like to address in this chapter.

Conversion cries out for a culture, presumably a people, that will nurture the process. So many people, who are at least on registration cards as members of the parish, are in some phase of a human experience that could become a conversion experience, or the experience of being born again. The process is aborted, however, because of the absence of positive faith-filled mentoring, sponsoring, companioning figures. So often, then, a potential conversion experience is written off as bad luck, life dealing a bad hand, a bad roll of the metaphysical dice. Yet, it could very well be that God is self-revealing; God is communicating truth through such experiences. But the divine self-communication is missed for want of a translator, a mediator, a sacramental presence representing God and the faith community.

I believe a great deal of the mediation and mentoring needed for conversion can be done in small groups, or communal organisms in the parish. But we must keep in mind that a significant number of parishioners will not engage in intentional small groupings. Operating in parish life is the "wedge theory" that we discussed in the section on the Communal Parish project section. The widest, most densely populated part of the wedge is that which represents level-one parishioners—people who, developmentally, by personal choice, or because of personal restrictions or limitations, have a very basic, minimal kind of involvement or connection with parishes. Some in this category will feel an affinity with the parish despite their minimal involvement. But others run the risk of really falling through the cracks, with only a notional, cultural bond with the faith community.

The presence of people of faith, pastors with a small *p*, are crucial for the conversion process. Thus, I feel compelled to underscore and serve as an advocate for a ministry I have been involved in for twenty years, but which still gets very low priority in most parishes—that is proactive reach-out, especially to nominal, marginalized members.

As I state several times in this study, I believe that the Movement for a Better World's New Image of Parish is onto a truth when they state we are structured for failure, or at least poor results in terms of evangelization and reach-out. While small communities may be an ideal that we move toward, I do not believe evangelical reach-out is just an ideal but rather a pressing need. As stated earlier, NIP contends that the program-organization parish is structured for the average of 25 percent active members while 75 percent potential but inactive members go ignored. We continue in a mode, each year, of the maintenance of the status quo, ignoring the need to set mission-oriented goals.

In *Growing Plans*, evangelical pioneer Lyle Schaller lists some of the characteristics of a church committed to mission and growth: a staff that speaks of mission growth in both tone and size; a marketing plan to get the congregation into the consciousness of many people; a physical plant that is attractive, accessible, adequate for pastoral needs; and both pastoral and lay visitation of homes. Kennon Callahan in *Effective Church Leadership* and *Twelve Keys to an Effective Church* encourages congregations to emphasize being proactive, relational, intentional, and missional, rather than reactive, organizational, passive, and institutional. Developing the seminal notion mentioned earlier, "evangelization as paying attention," let us tease out even more how to be pastorally present to people in their moments of conversion readiness.

• *The neighborhood minister:* I have experienced this ministry being done in several ways. Some parishes have trained parishioners to serve as contact people for ten to fifteen households, with visitation of homes taking place quarterly. During such visits information about the parish is disseminated, as well as deep listening to the felt joys, needs, and wounds of parishioners. Eventually it is hoped that a rapport is developed between the neighborhood minister and those visited that will lead to a greater connectedness between the individual household and the larger parish. While quarterly visits may be sufficient to many, those in need, namely the elderly, sick, shut-in, the unemployed usually need more frequent visitation. The neighborhood minister is a connecting person between those visited and the services/ministries of the neighborhood and parish.

He or she is an evangelizer in the sense of being an entry-level, diagnostic type of servant leader especially attentive to the marginalized. This minister needs training in basic human-relations skills and the types of people who tend to engage in drop-out patterns.

• *The target-area service team:* Some parishes use the same kind of training to prepare a service team whose reach-out skills can be used in an ad hoc sort of way in many different areas of the parish. In effect, they move from area to area in a parish, doing visitation similar to that of the neighborhood minister, but in a less frequent way, alternating their services through different areas or sections of the parish. Their services may be employed in several areas of a parish, based on perceived need, in preparation for some parish event, like a mission, a parish assembly, or an adult education event, or some other function. Because these ministers' visits are only occasional and serve a given task or event, the rapport or trust between visitor and household is not as crucial as in a process of regular visitation. Many using this style of visitation also make the visits ecumenical in nature, visiting all homes in a target area. Visiting Protestant, or non-Catholic homes, the callers can either point nonpracticing Protestants to a church of their denomination or origin in the area, or serve as a threshold for entrance into the Catholic parish's precatechumenate. These ministers can also point nonpracticing Catholics toward the parish's process of reentry or reconciliation.

• *The telephone minister:* In another book, *Parishes That Excel*, I wrote about a parish in Schaumburg, Illinois, Church of the Holy Spirit, that has employed trained parishioners and a bank of telephones in the lower level of the parish center. Holy Spirit was following the lead of some Protestant congregations in using one of the communication tools of the age to reach out to and connect with people. Parishes using this model often use the broad ecumenical sweep described in the target visitation section above. Proponents of this strategy contend that a phone conversation is a much less threatening relational experience than an encounter in one's home. Holy Spirit and others using this technique report good numbers in terms of marketing success or attracting often noninvolved people to parish events and processes.

• *The sponsor figure in sacramental catechesis:* In describing the Communal Parish project, we discussed how level two of the project encourages participants to re-imagine sacramental catechesis through the process lens of the catechumenate, that is, in all sacramental preparation, participants are experiencing a journey of conversion. That journey ideally takes place in the context of a group or a cluster of various households. Not mentioned in that section is the importance of discerning, raising up, and training parishioners to serve as sponsor figures for individuals and households who are making that sacramental journey. I have consulted with both Catholic and Protestant congregations that were trying this mentoring/companioning kind of process with individuals and families in preparation for infant Baptism, First Communion and/or Reconciliation, Confirmation, and Marriage. In ways negotiated uniquely in every parish, sponsors/mentors are trained for a ministry of presence, listening, faith-sharing, prayer, elements of spiritual direction, and question-answering. The sacramental sponsor becomes the "Christian friend" who has "grandmother" or extra time to give to the person on the journey. Such sponsor figures have also been used effectively in mystagogical-type continuation ministry. After the sacramental moment, "where are they now?" Trained sponsor figures could/should be available to pursue that question and those people.

• *The reach-out potential of the worshiping assembly:* Evangelical churches, committed to church growth, highlight the evangelizing potential of the ordinary Christian. They encourage those who attend worship services to imagine themselves as missionaries. Most of the congregation must know nonpracticing members. The ordinary Christian ought to take the initiative and relationally bond with the unchurched or nonpracticing family member, coworker, or neighbor. The active member ought to try to have the courage simply to give witness to the difference Christ and the church make in his or her life. Then, the congregation is encouraged to both invite and companion the invitee to church services and other events. Though there are not longitudinal studies documenting the long-range commitment of people subscribing to evangelical churches via this strategy, the initial reports of success are astounding. This technique or strategy taps into the "reach-out through contagion" praxis of the early church and contemporary recovery programs.

• *Other people who could be made mission-sensitive:* There are many people who could participate in the mission-outreach dimension of the parish, rather than just engaging in their particular ministry that maintains the status quo of parish life. *Ushers,* or hospitality ministers, at weekend Masses eventually get a good idea of the "regulars" at a liturgy, and could become great resources regarding those who have dropped out. *Friends* of people experiencing either struggles or alienation from the parish could be encouraged in an ongoing way to notify appropriate ministers at the parish regarding a need for pastoral assistance. *Financial or stewardship administrative personnel* could certainly take note of a change in a person's donation patterns that might in turn indicate a problem or difficulty in a parishioner's life. Many evangelical churches operate out of the conviction that the parish ought to have a strategy to discern anyone (who is regular in worship) who suddenly misses three or more times. That person is to be called or visited without delay. This allows pastoral workers immediately to repair the hole in the evangelical net of intersecting staff and congregational relationships.

Let us keep in focus what all this potential relational coverage or restructuring is about. It is not an attempt to create yet another bureaucratic, hierarchical overlay over parishioners' or peoples' lives. In the chapter on conversion and in this chapter we are emphasizing that ordinary human experience most often serves as the trigger experience for growth and conversion. But ordinary experience can be "hard to read," "hard to listen to" without the assistance of another person of faith, or without the feeling tone of invitation, concern, and welcome exuding from a local faith community. Several main strategies have been suggested in this chapter for extending pastoral presence, in a decentralized way, off of staff and campus, to the reality of people's lives. The goal of evangelization is always facilitating conversion and Reign of God living. Ideally that is not the work of a few professionals but rather the responsibility of all. We need to restructure for the mission of pastoral presence to people's conversion readiness.

The Nominal Christian:
Concerns and Strategies

*I*n this chapter I will address more specifically than I have up to this point one of the most crucial questions facing the Catholic Church in terms of evangelization: the growing number of Catholics who are inactive in the church. It is important to keep in mind the vision from the previous chapter—that in generating new structures for the inactive member, we are trying to provide presence of moments of possible conversion. Their inactivity stems from many different reasons, as we shall see—from boredom with what goes on in their parishes, to hurt and anger, to either their own spiritual hunger that leads them elsewhere, or their spiritual malaise that leads them either to their beds or recreation and hobbies on Sunday mornings.

In his classic *The Unchurched American* (1988), George Gallup noted a rise in two categories of religious sentiment and behavior among mainline Protestants and Roman Catholics. On the rise is the number of people who consider themselves religious or spiritual, people of faith with a prayer life. But also on the rise is the number of people who say that they do not need a religious institution or faith community to support their faith or to offer moral guidance. Gallup named the phenomenon "the crisis of believing vs. belonging." He made several recommendations to the church on possible ways to address these trends. We will look at them later.

Concern for the nonpracticing, inactive member is not just a "numbers game." The huge number of baptized-sacramentalized nonbelongers is antithetical to the theological foundations of our church. Our faith is incarnational: we believe that the presence of the Risen One and the Holy One's self-revelation takes place not in the dominant culture's preoccupation with independence, but in community. From the creation accounts of Genesis to the Reign of God preaching of Jesus, the Scriptures cry out for a world characterized by communion, union with God and one another. Our faith is Trinitarian—as God is many but one, so any church claiming life in God's Spirit ought to try to imitate that Trinitarian model.

Catholic sacramental theology, heavily influenced now by the ongoing development of the catechumenate, is calling us away from a praxis of giving and receiving sacraments as "holy things." Sacramental moments are rather vows and pledges to God and community, as one is gradually initiated into and continually matures in the community. Recent ecclesiology, influenced by liberation theology, has challenged us to re-imagine church on several levels: the assembly, the basic ecclesial community, and the domestic church of home. Stewardship studies are revealing that parishes cannot squeeze any more financial resources out of the middle-aged or senior citizens. There is an untapped wellspring of ministerial gifts as well as financial resources in the huge numbers of people now estranged in some way from the community.

Despite this common-sense and theological perspective, mainline Protestant and Catholic churches continue to systematically "screen out," as Dr. John Savage so aptly puts it in *The Apathetic and Bored Church Member,* their nonpracticing members. Savage and the author of this book have for years tried to challenge parishes out of their "screening-out" postures and tendencies. Paulist Jac Campbell, who has developed a healthy strategy for ministering to inactives entitled *Landings,* lamented recently at a Chicago gathering that inactive Catholics are the biggest subpopulation in a parish. Yet ministry to them is not even a line item on the budget in a parish; a budget is revelatory of vision, values, and pastoral praxis.

One of the pioneers of the evangelical church movement, Lyle Schaller, in one of his eminently practical books, *Growing Plans,* says that any church that is interested in missionary outreach to the inactive and unchurched should invest at least 5 percent of its yearly budget to marketing the parish and its services. He also says there ought to be a system for monitoring attendance at worship and church functions. I referred to this in the last chapter. Any regular member who is absent for period of three weeks or more should receive a visit from a trained parishioner to reconnect with that member and heal wounds that may have developed.

Concern about inactive members, nominal-cultural faith, ineffective religious education and pastoral efforts have a history in Catholic circles as well. In the 1950s Pierre Liege prophetically spoke of the spiritual and cultural Catholics he saw in the church in Europe. He and Alfonso Nebrada were the most vocal in the preconciliar years in calling for a back-to-basics preevangelization and evangelization effort. In contrast to Vatican I, which in its documents used the term *gospel* once and never spoke of evangelization, Vatican II documents used the words *gospel* 157 times, *evangelize* 18 times, and *evangelization* 31 times. *Lumen gentium, Ad gentes, Christus Dominus, Presbyterorum ordinis* and *Apos-*

tolicam acutositatem speak of the responsibility of the People of God, religious, priests, and bishops to play their part in the missionary-evangelization activity of the church.

Throughout the 1950s, 1960s, 1970s, and 1980s, master-catechist Johannes Hofinger called for a refocusing of catechesis around basic evangelization themes, and a refocusing of such evangelizing-catechizing activities on adults rather than children. Hofinger felt the Catholic Church's preoccupation with children's religious education and the church's practice of distributing sacraments without discernible conversion were robbing the church's religious education efforts of any power.

Pope Paul VI's *Evangelii Nuntiandi* (1975) was and is obviously the touchstone document of the modern evangelization movement in the Catholic Church. After highlighting the beneficiaries of a renewed effort at evangelization (the active, the unchurched, the inactive, youth, victims of social injustice, those heavily influenced by contemporary media), he concludes the encyclical by speaking of evangelization as the basic feature or mission of the church as we approach a new millenium.

More recently, John Paul II has been calling for a "new evangelization." He first used this phrase on March 9, 1983, at Port-au-Prince, Haiti, speaking to the bishops of Latin America. He suggested especially that, with the arrival of 1992, five hundred years of evangelization will have taken place in the Americas. The year 1992 was highlighted as a benchmark year for evangelization with new vigor, techniques, and methods. The new evangelization includes a need for the re-evangelization of those people and countries presumably already evangelized.

Most recently, the National Conference of Catholic Bishops approved *Go and Make Disciples: Shaping a Catholic Evangelizing People*. This document is a national plan and strategy for Catholic evangelization in the United States. The document articulates three goals with suggested strategies:

(1) bring about in all Catholics such an enthusiasm for their faith that in living their faith in Jesus, they freely share it with others;

(2) invite all people in the United States, whatever their social or cultural background, to hear the message of salvation in Jesus Christ so they may come to join us in the fullness of the Catholic faith;

(3) foster gospel values in the American culture, promoting the dignity of the human person and the common good of our society, so that our nation may continue to be transformed by the saving power of Jesus Christ.

In addition, recent years have seen the generation of *Here I Am, Send Me: A Conference Response to the Evangelization of African Americans, The National Black Catholic Pastoral Plan,* and the *National Plan for Hispanic Ministry.* In these documents, reach-out and sensitivity to the un-churched or inactive members are also articulated.

Yet these episcopal, ecclesial pronouncements have yet to wake "the sleeping giant," as Gallup refers to the Catholic Church, to its responsibility to better minister to inactive members. Perhaps most telling is a large diocese in this country that has named evangelization its number one priority. One course in evangelization, which includes analysis of and strategies for the inactive member, is offered in the major seminary. It is an elective course. The fact that the "number one priority" is a seminary "elective" reveals the visionary and strategic paralysis that we are in relative to this most serious pastoral issue.

We will proceed to look at the "inactive opportunity" in four parts:

- why they are inactive;

- evangelization as paying attention;

- ministries of reconciliation; and

- spiritually awakening baby boomers; becoming mission-oriented parishes.

Categories of Inactive Members

Over the years, I have tried to describe many people who have left the church. In training programs for reach-out to the inactive Catholics around the world, I have spoken of:

- anti-institutionalists: Many of these people see hierarchy as all caught up in the maintenance of the ecclesiastical status quo;

- the locked out: Many Catholics perceive subjectively that sexual orientation, marital status, or some other situation has a priori excluded them from church membership and participation;

- nomadic people: Catholics and Americans in general move a great deal, and sociologically do not sink deep roots in neighborhood or church;

- those reacting to noncredible teachers: Many Catholics react negatively to what is perceived as the increasingly noncredible teaching authority of the hierarchy. The crucial font of this issue was the promulgation of *Humanae vitae*;

- angry Catholic women: Many Catholic women are resisting the institutionalized sexism of the institutionalized church;

- the tired drop-out: Many generous, good-hearted people have burned out in volunteer ministry and "do-foring" for a priest or staff, never feeling appreciated or thanked;

- the lifestyle drop-out: Some have values and behaviors that have taken them far from the church or the Reign of God;

- the spiritually needy drop-out: Some claim that their church of origin fails to feed them spiritually. This group often gravitates to evangelical megachurches, now present around the world. Some simply stay in bed on Sunday morning. Others have reinvested in some other organization that is spiritually nurturing, e.g., Twelve Step programs, the New Age movement, etc.;

- the racial ethnic drop-out: Many Hispanics and Asians feel unwelcomed in the large, anonymous, often English-speaking Roman Catholic assembly. Many of these people are attracted by the doctrinal fundamentalism, love-bombing, and highly participative style of cults, sects, and evangelical groups;

- the truly alienated: Many Catholics genuinely have been hurt by some church person and/or event. Often these people discover other layers or stories of pain from different people and seasons of their lives;

- the scandalized: Recent press and media attention regarding hierarchy and clergy have left faithful Catholics shocked and horrified. Capuchin Michael Crosby is one who feels the pedophilia issue is a wound from which the image of the clergy and church may not recover;

- the prophetically alienated: Some have left active church participation to stand against official church policy that they perceive as not of Christ and the gospel;

- the unawakened, the sacramentalized unawakened: Whether formally initiated into the church or not, these people, often young adults, have never had a major conversion experience that would lead them to any degree of church participation.

This list is certainly not exhaustive. But of growing concern to this author are the spiritual drop-outs, among whom there are many young adults; the unawakened, also highly populated by young adults; and racial-ethnic group drop-outs. Penny Lernoux, before her death, lamented the huge number of Catholics in Latin America and also in the United States who have been proselytized away from their church of origin. Similarly, Allan Figueroa Deck projects that the drain-off of Hispanics from American Catholic parishes will continue. The absence of an indigenous clergy, failure on the part of parishes to do inculturation well, and the lack of readiness on the part of the American Catholic parish to do multicultural ministry all are contributing factors. Deck fears the loss of Hispanics will be a loss to the church that could well last for centuries.

Evangelization as Paying Attention

In a pastoral reflection on the loss of Hispanics to proselytizers, the bishops of Baja, California, stated that the typical parish, as it is set up today, does not have adequate struc-

tures for evangelization. They then gave a very simple conno-
tation to evangelization. They said evangelization is "paying
attention to people." Most parishes do not have adequate
structures to pay attention to their potential congregation.
As Catholic parishes fail to pay attention, well-scripted,
trained lay proselytizers from other denominations do not
miss the opportunities. Catholics falling through the cracks
of their own parishes are often readily picked up by one of
many evangelical churches. The bishops made several recommendations for addressing this anonymity problem:

(1) The large parish ought to be broken down into more
manageable sections, with the baptized trained to
oversee the sections.

(2) The sections should gradually move toward the generation of small base communities, again with the baptized trained to pastor the small communities.

(3) Every parish should have some sort of regular program
for calling on parishioners or engage in home
visitation.

In essence, the bishops were saying the typical Catholic
congregation is not adequately pastored, because the pastoring of thousands of people is put on the shoulders of one
canonically appointed male celibate priest and his meager
staff. They were suggesting that pastoring, in the sense of
shepherding and mentoring, must be multiplied by sharing
it with the community. The community must accept responsibility for pastoral care of its members.

This pastoral reflection reechoes some of the wisdom of
the New Image of Parish Project of the Movement for a
Better World. NIP, as it is popularly known, contends that
a typical parish is a collection of anonymous strangers. They

set forth the following statistics as reflective of most parishes around the world. In the average parish only about 5 percent are actively involved in ministry, leadership, or any felt sense of community. Another 20 percent join the 5 percent in eucharistic worship on weekends; and so, about 25 percent participate in Mass on the weekends. Seventy-five percent of the typical congregation is functionally unchurched. They may be baptized or otherwise sacramentalized, but they are far from the church.

NIP teaches that parishes need to develop strategies and structures for better reach-out, communication, and faith nurturance. The first suggestion is that considerable time be given to the "Call to All." The "Call to All" is an intensive reach-out to all potential parishioners through home visitation, retreats, missions, and adult education in an effort to nudge parishioners toward a shared vision of church, a common ecclesiology. NIP also stresses the importance of sectioning the parish and training parishioners to pastor the sections. Ideally, in these sections, groupings are arranged. Groups are simply social gatherings at which people are given the opportunity to meet one another and bond and engage in months and years of faith formation. Hopefully, groupings will lead some to make a further commitment to small Christian communities. Parishioners would obviously need training for pastoring such groups. Finally, another pastoring figure, called a messenger, is trained for regular home visitation of ten to fifteen households.

St. John Neumann parish in Eagen, Minnesota, is experimenting with NIP-like structures. Through a neighborhood-minister training program they hope to effect better one-to-one reach-out and communications. Through an ever-evolving small community process they seek to provide deeper faith nurturance for those who want it.

A special interest of mine has been the training of people for home visitation. While attempted in various styles over the years, the most effective method seems to be the "precinct-captain" model, wherein trained parishioners take the responsibility to visit a specific number of homes in their area at least quarterly. In these visits to practicing and non-practicing alike, much can be done at least to start the conversation with an alienated or inactive member. Training for this ministry involves practice in human–relations skills. Methods for doing such training can be found in my book *The Evangelizing Parish* and in my *Reaching Out,* an audio-cassette series.

Realizing the extent of alienation from the church in Scotland, Archbishop Thomas Winning of Glasgow is encouraging parishes to come up with new structures that include a home visitor for every ten families, a monthly newsletter to every registered household (presuming many are inactive), and regular special events to welcome nominal Catholics back.

George Gallup, writing in *The Unchurched American* and reflecting on better ministry to those alienated from the church, stressed the importance of providing people with rich religious experiences (over institutionalization), reach-out to and formation of adults (over preoccupation with children), opportunities for gathering in small groups, and of more one-on-one reach-out. What is interesting in the Baja statement, the work of NIP, the Glasgow project, and Gallup's recommendation is that all concur in calling for a radically new way of doing parish, one that stresses the relational and communal over programs and volunteer ministries.

Ministries of Reconciliation

Besides restructuring for "paying attention," some parishes have begun very deliberate ministries of reconciliation to the inactive—especially to those who have been hurt in some way by a church event or person. Years ago, Father John Forlitti of Minneapolis-St. Paul began a process called *Alienated Catholics Anonymous*. John would get the word out in various ways—pulpit announcements, newspaper ads, word of mouth—that he was having a series of dinners, which he himself would cook, for those who have been away from the church. His experience with this ministry is recorded in his audiotape *Love in the Food*. At the sessions, people would largely ventilate their often angry feelings about past encounters with the church.

The same title is being used by Father Thomas Cahalane of Mother of Sorrows Church in Tuscon, Arizona. Tom's approach includes a time for ventilation of hurt or frustration, but also opportunities for catechetical update on sacraments, human sexuality, the changing church, divorce and annulments. Both expressions of Alienated Catholics Anonymous encourage a celebration of sacramental reconciliation and a return to the eucharistic table. Tom Cahalane uses the highly attended Christmas and Easter Masses to announce the beginning of the series, which runs for six weeks. In effect, he says to the large congregation: "I know many of you are not here regularly; but you are always welcome. And if you feel the urge to return soon, Alienated Catholics Anonymous is beginning in a few weeks."

An internationally recognized effort at reconciliation with inactive Catholics came out of the North American Forum on the Catechumenate. It is called "Re-membering Church." It was begun in response to the admonition of Cardinal Joseph Bernardin that a sense of process be restored to reconciliation. The re-membering process is a reechoing of the church's ancient Order of Penitents. Resembling the catechumenate, it includes an evangelization period, a ritual of beginning, a time for formation, an actual entering of the Order of Penitents during Lent, sacramental absolution and a public return to the eucharistic table on Holy Thursday, and a follow-up mystagogical-like stage. Reflecting the most recent thinking on the catechumenate, the re-membering process is offered year round.

While there is much value in the *re-membering church* processes, which include profound healing and liberating experiences for people, in Chicago and other places around the country there has been some difficulty in pastorally implementing the model. Many returning Catholics that I have worked with have reacted negatively toward having to take such a lengthy time to return to the church (often up to a year). They have also reacted negatively to being labeled "penitents," when often it seems as if the church has hurt them, that the church ought to be "penitent." Many did not like public rituals during which their alienation and return are trumpeted before the entire liturgical assembly.

For the above reasons, I put together another Chicago-based model called "The Reconciling Parish." The essence of this model is contained in a book of the same name produced by Tabor Publishing in 1990. The Reconciling Parish process involves a period of outreach, followed by gatherings of those who have been attracted by the reach-out and the advertising. Initial meetings are devoted to much story-sharing regarding reasons that people have for growing alienated from the church. In addition, ten topics of a catechetical nature are included in the process. The topics are credal in nature. They are:

(1) We believe in the face of mystery.

(2) We believe in God (parent), Creator of heaven and earth.

(3) We believe in Jesus, born of Mary.

(4) We believe in Jesus who was crucified, died, and was buried.

(5) We believe in the Holy Spirit, the Lord, the giver of life, who proceeds from the Father and the Son.

(6) We believe in one, holy, Catholic and apostolic Church.

(7) We believe in Baptism and the other sacraments.

(8) We believe in the forgiveness of sin.

(9) We believe in the resurrection of the dead.

(10) We believe in the life of the world to come.

The Reconciling Parish suggests a catechetical methodology for each credal statement. Participants are asked to keep a journal on some questions to help discern their starting point. Discussion in small groups follows among participants and their sponsors if the latter are included in the process. A personal witness talk on the topic follows, as well as a teaching on the topic. A second journal activity follows the talks, to chart possible change or movement because of the talks. Then there is some large group sharing, or one-on-one sharing with a sponsor or companion figure. The sessions end with an appropriate Scripture reading and prayer.

This process can be so arranged to lead into a Holy Thursday celebration of return. The Reconciling Parish does not single out returnees as penitents. Instead the whole parish is encouraged to take on the posture of penitents during Lent.

I already mentioned Church of the Holy Spirit's innovative telephone evangelization strategy. They have placed a bank of phones in the basement of the parish center and trained close to one hundred parishioners to call ten thousand households in close proximity to the parish. The script of the phone call was designed to find out if the person being called was involved in any local parish or church. If the person was already active in a parish community, the caller simply let them know that Church of the Holy Spirit was in the area and ready to be of service. What should be noted is the follow-up process Holy Spirit created for those in need of reconciliation.

If the person called indicated they were not involved in any parish, the offer was made to send them more information. Out of over nine thousand completed calls, nine hundred people expressed interest in receiving more information. A list of these people was kept and they were invited to a variety of series. One was particularly targeted to those who had questions about what it means to be Catholic, and to those who have been away who sought to return. *"Once a Catholic"* is a six-part series resembling those described for Alienated Catholics Anonymous. The series concludes at the baptismal font, with participants making a recommitment to their Baptism.

Several parishes in Naperville, Illinois, have worked together on homecoming evenings. Literally hundreds of people have come to these evenings, largely advertised in local newspapers. Upon arrival at the appointed church, participants can go to different parts of the building for different services—to talk about annulment, to seek guidance and counseling, or to celebrate sacramental reconciliation. As best as it can be done, follow-up ministries are offered to people in need of such care.

Many parishes around the country are also experiencing success in ministry to inactives by better efforts at welcoming newcomers to the parish. Rather than the impersonal signing of a card, registration becomes a process of learning about the parish and covenanting with the parish. Similarly, many parishes are using sacramental catechesis processes around First Eucharist and First Reconciliation, like those described in Year Two of the Communal Parish Project, as effective times to encourage nonpracticing parents to return to the church to support their children in faith. Reframing sacramental catechesis along the steps and rhythm of the catechumenate, and including parents in the journey, have been quite successful. Similar efforts are being made for baptismal preparation and marriage preparation.

Spiritually Awakening Baby Boomers: Becoming Mission-Oriented Parishes

In his book *Effective Church Leadership*, Dr. Callahan says that Christian churches locked in a maintenance mode will continue to decline in numbers. Mission churches that place an emphasis on all the baptized being missionaries for the Reign of God will be successful, he says. One such mission-oriented church is Willow Creek Community Church in South Barrington, Illinois. I mention it here as an example of a larger phenomenon, the evangelical megachurch movement that passionately seeks out the nonpracticing members of other churches. The number of former Catholics now part of Willow Creek's methodology is to convince the practicing churchgoer to become a missionary. Each member is trained in a seven-step strategy:

- build a relationship with someone who is unchurched;

- at an appropriate time share a verbal witness about your faith;

- invite the unchurched person to a basic–seeker service, which is oriented toward people just beginning to wonder about faith;

- gradually invite that person to a believer's service, which is of greater depth and intensity and occasionally involves the Lord's Supper, or Communion;

- invite the now–active member into a small Christian community;

- help the new member to discern gifts he or she can bring to the community in ministry;

- finally, well into the process, invite the new member to responsibly steward his or her financial resources to the community.

The attitude shift from maintenance to mission, the seven-point missionary strategy mentioned above, and the relevant programs that touch people in the reality of their lives in these evangelical megachurches may seem simplistic to us. But the numbers of baby boomers attracted to these churches give evidence to their effectiveness. Sociologist Wade Clark Roof predicts a trend among some baby boomers (born between 1946 and 1964) to return to a church—but not necessarily their church of origin. Roof, in a *Generation of Seekers*, divides this huge demographic group into three categories: loyalists, who have never left their church of origin; returnees, who are coming back to the same church; and dropouts, who will continue in alienation patterns. Across all three categories, there are common drives: the quest for spirituality and meaning, a renewed zeal for belonging, and a felt need for spiritual roots for family. I would add a fourth, the need for inner healing. They will attend a congregation where these needs are met. Writing in a recent issue of *America,* a young man said that he left the Catholic Church because he felt Christ was eclipsed by the institution and other things. At an evangelical mission-oriented church, he met Christ and felt community for the first time.

Perhaps the real problem in all this is that Catholic leaders and people continue with Sunday Mass and parish programs, oblivious to both the problem and the opportunity of ministering to inactive members like boomers. A young pastor recently told me after a presentation on becoming mission parishes: "Ideally, I agree with everything you have suggested. But my energies are consumed with maintenance activities. I do not have time for mission." The "practicing," "active" church is really "inactive" when it comes to missionary responsibility. Perhaps things still look too good: the parking lot and pews are relatively full on weekends; the collection is at least respectable. The Roof research, as well as Robert Withrow's recent study *Sharing the Journey,* suggests that new strategies of encouraging the congregation to evangelize, passionate and contemporary worship with upbeat music and good preaching, the opportunity for meeting in small groups, and opportunities for pastoral counseling and multiple healing ministries are vital missionary strategies for reaching this age group.

A real pastoral concern is that neither priests nor other pastoral staff members have been trained in the skills needed for such a future church. Perhaps dioceses ought to take some time out to be resourced in some common skills and strategies for doing "mission church." Maybe we do not try because we do not know how to try. Most parish leadership needs significant retooling to actualize what is called for in this book.

In its excellent binder of material on working with inactive people, "Stephen Ministries" says something that pastoral leaders in the Catholic Church need to take to heart. When it comes to inactive members, there is much that can be done. Maintenance ministry is safe and comfortable. Mission ministry and ministries of reconciliation are unpredictable and therefore often avoided.

I attended a gathering recently at which Woman Church, Corpus, and other independent church-related groups were present. Many spoke of being beyond hurt, anger, and alienation. Deeply rooted in Catholic identity, they are committed to addressing issues like married clergy, the ordination of women, and other issues of justice-doing, rather than waiting and seeking permission.

Some standards of integrity are needed for such doing; about this there was general agreement. But there was also general agreement that Catholics who genuinely love the church can no longer tolerate anemic leadership, decline, and decay.

9

Ministry in the Communal Parish

*M*inistry consists of being and/or doing. Ministry employs or uses gifts of the Holy Spirit that are present, if incipient, in every person. The goal of ministry is always to further usher in and facilitate God's Reign, that elusive, expansive reality spoken of at the beginning of this book, which was the mission of Jesus. The Kingdom is now, or ought to be, the mission of the church. The rite of entrance into God's Reign is personal and communal conversion. Evangelizing ministry facilitates such conversion. Ministry is always oriented toward conversion. At least it should be.

But recent decades of calling the baptized to ministry have too often been expressions of volunteerism more than the kind of ministry that we have been envisioning. At Holy Family parish where I work, the staff frequently uses the term *do-fer* to speak of the volunteerism that we seek to get away from. "Do-fering" refers to people volunteering to "do for" the pastor, the D.R.E. or the youth minister to help someone who "really" has the responsibility to minister. In this view the baptized at best help out rather than actualize their own vocation and ministerial responsibility.

The aversion to this "do-ferism" on our part has led us as a staff to much more seriously develop a spirituality of stewardship. Finances are only a minimal part of an expanded view of stewardship. Stewardship involves a discerned awareness of one's core calling in life, how one has been gifted by the Spirit, and how those gifts are best used for the Body of Christ, the church, and for God's creation, the world. We hope to foster and propagate this view of stewardship through the development of a school of ministry, which is offered in connection with opportunities for small communities.

I have been part of parish-based ministry-training program and schools of ministry for years. I have been convinced for years that ministerial training is best done "in the trenches," in the "grassroots," rather than through centralized diocesan lay-ministry training programs. The latter are oriented too much toward the processing of an elite core who respond to the call to ministry, rather than helping all the members of the congregation respond as stewards. Centralized lay-ministry training programs create a new breed of clerics, ministerial specialists. The parish-based school of ministry is an attempt to unleash the ministerial potential of the entire congregation.

In previous attempts at schools of ministry, however, it has been my experience to train people for specific skills, people who had already volunteered for ministry. While the good intentions of such people must never be doubted, and while the ministerial development of some in such programs might be exemplary, these programs nonetheless run the risk of preparing folks for enlightened "do-ferism." A school of ministry that reflects some of the vision and convictions of this book would look quite different from the lay-ministry training programs of the past. Ministerial efforts would follow a common discipline that would cut across all areas of parish expertise, harnessing people and charisms in an evangelical, missiological intentionality and praxis. Let us take some time to explore what such an enterprise might look like. Please note: some of the pieces of what follows need not be done independently by one parish. As I stated in another book, *Parishes That Excel*, it would be advantageous for contiguous parishes, or at least parishes that are moving in a common direction, to consider forming a pastoral alliance for excellence jointly to sponsor and fund different components of a school of ministry.

(1) I believe that the basic level of training that must occur in such a school is training in various skills of discernment. The most foundational of discernment efforts is to discern one's core calling in life, one's vocation. I believe that God has been calling each of us to a way of being and doing in the world from the moment of our conception. Each of us, with unique gifts and personality traits, has a contribution to make, something to offer, and also much to receive in life in God's Kingdom. Notice that the first movement in discernment is not to some possible task that one might perform in the church, but rather an assessment of God's call as it addresses the core of the person.

As I assess, discern my life, my mind frequently jumps to consider the roles that I presently hold or may hold in the future: associate pastor or pastor, coordinator of parish evangelization efforts, university professor, evangelization-center director, psychotherapist. Those tasks are not my core calling. I would certainly abort or make superficial any discernment process of my core calling if I stopped at any one of those tasks. For what if, through circumstances, one of those roles or tasks ceases to exist? Do I cease to exist? Or am I no longer called by God?

Of course not! All of us are constantly being called by God. Circumstances will change roles, the slots we hold. But the core calling endures, while it often changes in size or shape. We need times and places in parish life to give people the opportunity to discern on that level of being. If roles were stripped away from any of us, what would be the categorical imperative that would remain? As I look at my own life (not intending to be overly pious), I cannot imagine myself not being a man in pursuit of God, in pursuit of meaning, in need of healing, and eager to aid in the process of healing others through the grace of God. I cannot imagine myself not teaching, not counseling or mentoring. I cannot imagine myself not loving and remaining passionately committed to others in friendship and familial love. Those are some of the core callings of my life. In developing such a tract for parishioners, we need to pursue similar questions: What could you imagine not doing? What must you be and do? What do you uniquely bring to life? What does the world need from you? From parishioners other types of answers might come: fathering, mothering, being married, being single, creating, teaching, building, nursing, doctoring, working in service professions, and on and on. This kind of discernment lifts peoples' lives out of the sole pursuit of profit.

A second level of discernment-training involves the discernment of gifts. As mentioned earlier in this book, people in discernment of giftedness need to be given time alone to name their gifts of being (who they are) and doing (abilities they have from God to perform in certain ways). Having listened to themselves, they need to repeat their listening to others, presumably others who know them and who can react (affirm, confirm, challenge) to their "self-reporting." These "outer authorities" can likewise mention additional

gifts that perhaps the person "self-reporting" does not yet
see in himself or herself.

A third level of discernment that a school of ministry
might help with is the discernment of truth. In *Evangelization Today*, Bernard Häring prophetically lifts evangelization
out of the realm of programs to describe it as the pursuit of
morality and truth. In its posture of evangelizing, ministry
seeks to aid the spiritual pilgrim in assessing the images of
the dominant cultures, and critiquing them against the values and images of Jesus and his revelation of the Reign of
God. Time needs to be given especially to personal values/
dominant-image discernment, scrutinizing where one's own
personal value system is critiqued by the gospel and in need
of moral conversion.

Training in at least three levels of discernment, core calling, giftedness, and the pursuit of morality, seems to be an
integral first step in any serious ministerial training.

(2) A second level of such training might be one that parishes of similar evangelical, mission-oriented vision might
cosponsor and fund. This is a theological core. Minicourses
that ground ministers or stewards in our tradition could include: Jesus' vision of the Kingdom or the Reign of God,
the evolution of our convictions about Jesus, ecclesiology or
theology of church, how to read and use scripture, skills
in exegesis and hermeneutics, principles for contemporary
morality, history of our sacramental life, contemporary sacramental spirituality, issues in social justice, prayer and spirituality, and others discerned as needed as the school develops.
One standard course or minicourse that should be a require-
ment in the curriculum is a series on human-relations skills,
such as active listening, confrontation, conflict resolution,
encouragement, and a development of these skills for organizations and systems. The latter should include how to engage
in a time-managed, effective business meeting, how meet-

ings should rotate agenda to include, besides business, training (when needed) and faith formation.

It has been my approach in training to try to impart to stewards and ministers a standard discipline that all in ministry employ in their groups and organizations. This standard discipline involves the following:

• *Need discernment:* As mentioned earlier, in a wholistic vision of a parish cycle of evangelization, so also in all ministries and groups within a parish ministerial efforts or stewardship always begin with listening to needs and attempting to design ministerial strategies that respond to those needs. All ministers-stewards (religious education, worship, pastoral care, youth) need to be scrupulous about listening to and responding to needs.

• *Vision or mission statements:* What is the vision of the parish? How does the parish see itself uniquely accomplishing the mission to evangelize, the mission of the Reign of God? Many parishes' mission statements are useless because they were written by a small group of ideologues. Mission statements that are truly expressive of a parish's consciousness are participatory in nature. That is, in a step-by-step process, the input of all parishioners is systematically solicited in the quest for articulating a parish vision. The staff, the parish leadership council or community, the various boards of ministry, parish organizations, and ordinary parishioners who are invited to various listening and process sessions—all are invited to contribute to an evolving vision of the faith community. A representative editorial team pieces the input together meaningfully. Finally, the vision statement is liturgically promulgated at weekend Masses. The articulation of vision or mission should be deliberately participative and inclusive. In my experience, mission statements with substance take months to be completed. The process of doing such statements is an important exercise in parishioners "doing theology, doing ecclesiology" together. I believe an additional step is needed relative to these statements. Each ministry group, program, and organization within a parish needs also to articulate its sense of mission against the mission statement of the parish.

• *Goals and priorities; specific mission objectives:* the parish as a whole and each of its subgroups need to articulate reasonable goals and priories or mission objectives. These objectives ought to be designed to last for at least three years, with specific accomplishments targeted for each year. In addition, goals and objectives need to include missiological objectives, reaching out to nominal members and the unchurched.

• *Program design:* Having been serious about the first three steps highlighted here, ministries and organizations need to design strategic programming plans that are congruent with the articulated needs, mission, goals, and priorities.

• *Discernment of gifts and roles:* We really are taking the heart-values of the cycle of evangelization, mentioned earlier, and pushing them to the point of micromanagement. With a given ministry or organization, once the program design has been pronounced, there needs to be a discernment of gifts among those involved in the program. Based on the giftedness of people involved in the project, who is going to perform what roles?

• *Dissemination of tasks:* Discernment of gifts and roles naturally leads to a division of labor—who is going to do what to accomplish the long- and short-term goals articulated by a program or ministry?

• *Understanding and practicing enablement:* I have mentioned before that I do not think we who hold positions on parish staffs can empower people. The Spirit of God gives power, gifts, charisms to each individual. We in professional ministry can only finesse, facilitate, advance the cause of enabling the already empowered. Let us study again a model of enablement that I have found effective.

• *Time-lining:* Having set long-range goals and objectives, ministering communities and groups need to establish more short-term objectives, articulating *when,* in the next weeks and months, individuals will accomplish their responsibilities and tasks.

People in traditional seminary or ministry-training programs have been trained in the strategies of direct service:

• The professional minister/ministers

• to all people, individually, directly.

In an enablement model, the professional minister trains lay leaders and lay teams to minister to given target populations in the parish. Unlike the direct-delivery model (professional ministers ----> any/all people), the enablement model looks like this: professional minister ---> lay leaders ----> community of ministers -----> target populations (e.g., teens, children, families, etc.).

• *Climate control:* As Maslow taught us years ago, people only stay with organizations that help with their life needs of belonging, participation, and a feeling that they are held in esteem. Certainly the ministry leaders, but also all members of a ministry, group, or community ought to participate in creating an environment that encourages people to "stay with us."

• *Communication:* In any parish group or ministry, the operative rule of thumb is *communication*. You cannot communicate enough! Human-relations training teaches that most of us are poorly equipped in the skills of sharing emotions and convictions. Similarly, we often presume people know information that they simply do not. "Leave a paper trail," the experts tell us. In a parish, we need to do the same. Effective communication leads to a kind of transformational relating wherein the shared information between and among people creates a new reality/environment that did not exist before.

• *Evaluation and reshaping:* Evaluation is an important value and behavior that needs to be advanced in ministerial circles. We shy away from evaluation because we are uncomfortable with criticism or negative feedback. Evaluation is certainly a heart-value to be embraced. The findings of evaluation need to be embraced, assimilated, and used for reshaping any given ministry toward improvement.

• *Rooted in prayer and spirituality:* Individuals and groups need to contextualize all these skills in ongoing experiences of spiritual renewal, deepening one's prayer life, dedication to Scripture, discernment of God's call, emotional health, and groundedness in community.

(3) Having covered in detail one standard offering in the *core* of ministerial training, namely a standard discipline or approach to ministry, and having articulated also the theological core that would be part of this curriculum, let us move on to a third level of ministerial training or the school of ministry—the level of training electives.

The basic ministerial divisions of a parish may vary in terminology or how they are named, but they remain essentially the same. They are:

- Evangelization, catechesis, and religious education;

- Prayer, the spiritual life, liturgy;

- Pastoral care, ministry to the sick, various ministries to those broken or in crisis;

- Youth evangelization, catechesis, social ministry, spiritual direction, vocational discernment;

- Administration and stewardship: the nuts-and-bolts business ministries of a parish;

- Parish social life and social organizations and events;

- Social-justice concerns and outreach.

At Holy Family we ask each ministerial division to look into itself and name areas of need, concern, and development. Leaders in each division are to name elective mini-courses/events that would help their ministers-stewards grow in specific skills for their area of ministry.

(4) There is a fourth level that needs to emerge and develop in parish life. It is the area of mission to the marketplace. Seminars, workshops, minicourses, renewal experiences need to bear down on perhaps the most real dimension of ministry—not church and parochial ministries but rather those that bring Christ and the values of God's Reign to the real world—workplace, neighborhood, and family. Jesuit scholar John Haughey did groundbreaking reflections on this in his book *Converting Nine to Five*. Haughey poses the questions: How do we get beyond profit motivation in our work? How do we re-imagine work as vocation, all of us cocreating the world with God? Pastoral theologian-minister John Fontana confronted these issues in his long

years at the Center for Faith and Work at Old St. Patrick's Church in downtown Chicago.

We close with a reminder. While training may sound very Pavlovian or behavior modification-oriented in tone, ministerial training is indeed a deeply spiritual activity. It is the unleashing and intentional directing of the gifts of the baptized toward service. As I mentioned earlier, 50 to 75 percent of a parish staff's time ought to be given to this kind of activity.

10

Pastoral Planning as Planning for Evangelization

I was asked recently to conduct a series of sessions in a parish on future planning for evangelization. As I began the sessions, I was told by the pastor that a diocesan consulting team had been there the week before to get in motion a long-term pastoral planning process. I reported with no competitive edge that the people who attended the other sessions said that the evangelization planning session, which was reach-out and missiological in nature, made a lot more sense then the pastoral planning session. When I investigated that a bit further, the people reported that the pastoral planning team seemed intent on mandating new groups and structures that were to be created for the pastoral planning project, but it was not clear to the participants what those groups were to be planning for.

I was struck again by the compartmentalization mindset of many in church work. Or to put it more directly and clearly, how can a parish engage in pastoral planning without evangelization planning? Pastoral planning should be planning for the church's mission to evangelize.

We in church work need to learn from the business world how to do planning, or we need to bring people from the business world in to do it with pastoral input. Church folks often become lost in ideals and process, but fail to set tangible, measurable goals. Too often we throw out one-liners without the specific breakdown that would tell us who is doing what and when to achieve specific goals. I repeat here the therapeutic process for systems and organizations that I mentioned in the core curriculum for schools of ministry. All in leadership and ministry in a parish need to internalize these disciplines:

(1) need discernment

(2) vision or mission statements

(3) goals and priorities; specific mission objectives

(4) program design

(5) discernment of gifts and roles

(6) dissemination of tasks

(7) understanding and practicing enablement

(8) time-lining projects

(9) control of environment and relationships toward self-esteem and belonging needs

(10) communication

(11) evaluation and shaping

(12) deepening prayer life and spirituality

These disciplines need to be brought to bear on every part of an evangelization-pastoral plan.

I want to reemphasize the importance of time-lining projects. In evangelization and pastoral planning it is important to have both immediate-proximate and long-range measurable goals. For example, in moving toward some goals of the Communal Parish project discussed earlier, questions like the following need to be asked:

When is it reasonable to launch a pilot on small groups?

What needs to happen, piece by piece, to achieve this goal?

When should each piece of the process be completed?

When will the initial pilot be completed?

When and how will there be evaluation of the pilot?

When will we do innovation enhancement, in terms of expanding our offerings of small groups?

When will round two of small groups be offered?

When do we begin proximate preparation for round two and whatever enhancement of the project that may result from evaluation?

All of these are questions geared toward proximate preparation. There are, of course, the long-range time-lining questions that sound like these:

How many do we hope to have in small groups by 1995? 1996? 1997? 1998? 2000?—based on our experiences in 1993–1994, or whatever the year of the initial pilot?

How many parishioners do we hope to have in family-based and/or small group/catechumenate-like processes of sacramental catechesis by 1995? 1996? 1997? 1998? 1999? 2000?—based on our experiences in 1993–1994, or whatever the year of the initial pilot?

The twelve-step discipline with specific emphasis on measurable goals and time-lining, needs to be applied to each step of an evangelization-pastoral planning process.

Let us look at the key pieces of such a process in the setting of a large metropolitan diocese as it wrestles with long-range planning. The following are actual key pieces of a plan that a diocese is struggling with. The plan espouses many of the heart-values articulated in this book and in the Communal Parish project.

Glimpse of a Diocesan Pastoral Plan

This particular diocesan plan, articulated in 1993–1994, calls for the implementation of the goals of the United States bishops' national plan, *Go and Make Disciples*. To repeat, they are:

(1) To bring about in all Catholics such enthusiasm for their faith that, in living their faith in Jesus, they freely share it with others;

(2) To unite all people in the United States, whatever their social or cultural background, to hear the message of salvation in Jesus Christ, so they may come to join us in the fullness of Catholic faith;

(3) To foster gospel values in the American culture, promoting the dignity of the human person and the common good of our society, so that our nation may continue to be transformed by the saving power of Jesus Christ.

The diocese decided that for three years it would focus on the Bishop's first goal, and proposed decisions and actions that in measurable behavior would enflesh that first goal.

(1) Proposed decision: Within three years, structures will be established to facilitate the implementation of *reevangelization* efforts in each parish/institution of the diocese.

Action: By fall of 1994, the diocesan pastoral center will establish structures that will support listening sessions at parish and cluster levels that will show how parishes and clusters can improve services and why people have left and are leaving active membership. The sessions will result in annual renewal programs, especially for active church-going Catholics.

- Beginning in Lent of 1995, there will be the development of the beginning of small faith communities in all parishes and clusters, using models already in existence as starting points.

- By Pentecost of 1995, in each vicariate of the diocese there ought to be an area-wide plan for reach-out to young adults and inactive Catholics.

- During 1994 the communications office for the diocese will devise a plan for the better implementation of media-print, audio and video material, radio and TV to evangelize.

- Beginning in 1995 and extending for three years, a convergence of pastoral center offices will sponsor expected, ongoing trainings of bishops, priests, and deacons with a special emphasis on seminars in preaching.

(2) Proposed Decision: The educational mission of the church, characterized by message, community, service, and worship, will be implemented within three years.

Action: Over the next year and a half, every parish will cooperate in developing a deanery plan for the implementation of this plan. This plan will:

- give priority to efforts at adult faith-development;

- include youth ministry and youth catechesis;

- pay attention to multiculturalism;

- establish target goals for increasing the number of people participating in the educational mission on a yearly basis;

- provide for anchor schools, collaboratively supported by parishes of an area.

(3) Proposed Decision: In order to achieve the latter decision, structures, resources, and personnel will be in place to support its implementation.
Action:

- In order that deaneries become more effective pastoral alliances for excellence, there should be eight to ten parishes per cluster or deanery. The vicar in charge of regional services will oversee the rearrangement of deanery operations to achieve excellence in all ministries, especially education.

- A competent, responsible person will be discerned in each deanery within the next year, who will be responsible for the articulation and implementation of an educational plan for the deanery, with all parishes contributing to the vision, funding, and needed personnel.

- Over the next three years, training programs will be established to ensure excellence in service among catechists, parochial school teachers, principals, directors of religious education, adult educators, and coordinators of youth ministry.

- Every parish or cluster of parishes will have, within three years, a director/coordinator/animator of religious education–catechetical ministries.

- Within three years, the dynamics of the Order of Initiation will be employed to prepare all journeying toward sacramental moments in diocesan parishes.

- All religious education efforts, within three years, will be restyled around family consciousness, recognizing the diversity of styles of families.

- Parishes or clusters of parishes will ensure the implementation of quality adult religious education processes, which respect the most current research on principles of adult learning.

There are both facilitating and restricting forces in this brief glimpse of several pieces of a diocesan pastoral plan for evangelization. I believe the facilitating factors include its minimal reach. Rather than tackling all three of the United States bishops' goals for evangelization, the plan sets its sights on the most basic goal, namely, renewing the spiritual lives of those who claim to be Catholics. The inherent wisdom in this is that Catholic parishes are desperately in need of a renewal of identity before they can effectively reach out to welcome or evangelize inactive members or the unchurched. Another dimension that I find fascinating is that the plan focuses on heart-values on which an emerging, universal common sense, or the *sensus fidelium,* can converge.  Looked at generically these are: meaning, healing, and connection. Broken down more specifically, the heart-values include: the need for better and more religious experience at worship; more specific outreach to generation "X," or younger Catholics; listening to people especially around reasons for alienation from the church; small groups; family-based–alternative models of religious education; the Order of Initiation as a faith-formation paradigm for parish life; and the necessity of better efforts at adult faith-formation. The

People of God worldwide are talking about these issues as crucial for renewing and refounding church.

The implicit restricting force in the plan is that it can be perceived as top-down in its direction. I personally do not feel any plan for renewal or refounding pastoral life can come from a central pastoral office. Diocesan leaders can at best hold out heart-values, or promote certain directions or intentionality. A facilitating force within the plan is that much of the work of the plan would have to be micromanaged in a decentralized way on the level of vicariates, deaneries, or clusters of parishes. The principle of subsidiarity, or working renewal on the smallest possible scale or level, would demand transcending even deanery boundaries to focus on the smaller unit of parish. Within the parish, there would need to be further micromanagement, utilizing the twelve disciplines toward achieving measurable goals in all prioritized areas. Fine-tuning such a plan on the level of a vicariate or deanery, cluster, and parish, and allowing decentralized, smaller units to organically create their own plan will eventually and inductively move toward the renewal of the whole, or the diocese.

In the chapter about getting started in small groups, I spoke of a primordial need in any attempted systemic change to convince the people involved of the need for change. Certainly in trying to implement a pastoral plan for evangelization, which has diocesan, vicariate/deanery/cluster and parish dimensions, there will have to be much shared visioning, goal-setting, and "getting on the same page" on many different levels. A great deal of conversation among "opinion makers" on the three general levels mentioned is necessary for the successful implementation of such a plan. Also, great patience will need to be practiced around the vicariate/deanery/cluster and parish pilots as such a plan nudges a local church toward paradigm shift.

I have been talking lately about the need for the Catholic and mainline Protestant churches to become *generative* organisms. I have written and spoken frequently about the felt sense that many of us have in pastoral ministry that we are evangelizing-catechizing ineffectively, that, in effect, we are failing to pass on the Catholic Christian experience to the next generation. If we are truly concerned and interested in passing on our faith tradition, we need to look at our structures for doing church and doing parish. We can pass faith on to future generations only through the structures that we put into place now.

Traditional hierarchical models of planning and organizing have as their goal management by *control*. Management by control is the inherent danger in any top-down enforced pastoral plan. Peter M. Senge, in *The Fifth Discipline*, expresses great wisdom as he describes the kind of planning/organizing that needs to take place in the future for organizations. He speaks of organizations as "learning organizations" and pieces of the organization as "learning teams." Learning organizations and teams engage in *systems thinking*—a growing ability to analyze how organizational systems work, both on the level of "the forest," or whole system (diocese), and smaller units, or microworld (parish and intraparish units). The twelve internal disciplines for systems used in this book are a shorthand attempt at systems thinking. Senge also advocates "personal mastery" not so much a skills appropriation, but rather an ongoing enriching of personal vision, a focusing of energies, seeing life and reality objectively.

Senge urges organizations to get in touch with personal and corporate "mental models." In *Re-Imagining the Parish* and in *Parishes That Excel*, I spoke of a similar reality as dominant images. Mental models are convictions, assumptions, images that we have, in this case about organizations, that often have arisen from past experience and which, if not open to change and challenge, can cause an organization not to change and therefore not face the future well. Mental models often are in need of "metanoia," or changed thinking. The failure to do this results in corporate learning disabilities.

"Shared vision" is crucial to Senge's discipline, and he cautions that vision statements had better be articulations of genuine shared vision. Shared vision is a growing experience of consensual thinking and valuing within teams and organizations. Shared vision speaks of a corporate intentionality or direction. Vision statements have a passing value— the naming of a shared vision in a given time and space. But I believe with Senge that the vision needs to be growing and expanding, hopefully, even as a vision statement is articulated. Finally, vital to Senge's strategies is "team learning," wherein members break out of individual performance concerns to expand corporate performance abilities because of new-found synergism. Team learning also involves a shared ability to understand and transform corporate–personal mental models.

Any organization concerned about its future must forego bureaucratic needs for control to plan seriously for the best interests of the system or organization. Shared core values need to replace diseased, ineffective bureaucratic values. Key in Senge's vision is the interplay needed between *analyzing* and *transforming* mental models and systems-thinking. Much of this style of planning needs to be done on the level of microworld, emphasizing the importance of localness. The centralized organization articulates heart-values (e.g., small Christian communities), but then surrenders control to microplanning and management.

In local microworlds, there is a great opportunity for experimentation and learning. The microworlds of parish, clusters of parishes, vicariate, and deanery are valuable to the larger network of microworlds, that is, the large organization, in that they can be a source of great research, learning, and collective wisdom.

Thus, in doing evangelization-pastoral planning, centralized authority should articulate heart-values and then surrender control. Centralized leadership needs to re-imagine itself as responsible for "stewardship for the organization," facilitating and advocating heart-values, mission, and constantly evolving visions. Evangelization–pastoral planning in microworlds provides opportunities for reflective action. Such planning, on other hand, promotes reflection and action that leads first to team learning, and then an infusion of wisdom to the larger organization (e.g., the diocese). The Communal Parish project, discussed earlier, is an example of a pastoral alliance for excellence, a local microworld, taking a heart-value advocated by leadership and doing its own effective, local planning—always standing willing to infuse wisdom back to other parishes and the diocese as a whole.

Having tried to change parishes from "downtown" for years, I have had a conversion in more recent years. Central leadership can espouse core values, but it cannot dictate the specifics of a plan. That must be grown organically and locally.

11

The Magnet Parish, the Marketing Plan

I have been doing a private study with a young student who is specializing in youth ministry. At a recent meeting, she lamented that she had only four to five high school teens show up for the last team meeting. While social gatherings for ski trips and dances attract a lot of people, the core planning meetings or those with a more spiritual tone attract very few. I asked her how she advertised her Sunday night, "more spiritual" gatherings. She said she had put it in the bulletin as an announcement. I asked her how many teens she thought picked up, much less read, the parish bulletin. She honestly confessed that very few did so. We began a discussion on how better to market or get the word out about her youth events.

I asked her to re-imagine the five to ten young people who attend the Sunday night meetings with some regularity as a core team or community. They should be discipled in a spirituality and vision of youth ministry, along with some adult leaders who can help with the process. After an appropriate period of time, and with the help of the adults, teens and adults should be challenged to begin proactive reachout to other teens, inviting them into similar types of groups.

Ideally perhaps five to ten small groups can multiply from the core group. The possible size of such an organically growing group could range now from 50 to 100 teens, in small groups of 10, with adult supervision. The original core team could function as a kind of leadership group, harnessing the energies of the new groups to do the following: mail a flyer or brochure to each teen registered in the parish each month, announcing upcoming teen events; make sure each registered teen in the parish gets a personal phone call each month, inviting him or her to a teen event; have teens make announcements at weekend liturgies about upcoming teen events; place posters around the church and in local stores announcing upcoming teen events. I ended my little tutorial with the challenge that as small groups of teens form, they are to be given the vision of the importance of reach-out. Ideally groups will be reach-out organizations to un-churched teens, inviting them both to social events and also more intimate small group experiences.

I shared with this student a strategy for ministry to youth that I have used over the years with great success in several parishes. I have since reflected on the experience and written about it in *Full Cycle Youth Evangelization* (F.L.A.M.E.) As the young woman looked at the model, she mentioned, from her own background, that the strategy very much resembled techniques she is aware of in marketing. The young woman's comment reminded me of some days I spent with Tom Peters and his associates at his Skunk Camp in southern California. I was a member of a group of businessmen and women who had convened to learn how to make their companies more excellent. As individuals in the small groups introduced themselves, my anxiety mounted in my small group as my turn came closer and closer. I was a Catholic priest coordinating evangelization efforts in the Archdiocese of Chicago. What was I doing in this high-powered business gathering? I haltingly described the activities of the office that I was a part of:

- our attempts to renew the faith-life of active Catholics;

- our attempts to connect again with alienated Catholics or those bored or apathetic toward the church;

- our reach-out efforts in the catchumenate toward the unchurched;

- our experimentation with reach-out to young adults and adolescents.

Surprisingly the business people were quite interested in what I had to say, and they put a label on my efforts. They said, "You really are coordinating marketing efforts for your church." At the time, I did not have even a clue as to what they meant by marketing. They went on to explain marketing as awakening people to needs that they do not even know they have. In the case of ministry and evangelization, this consists of awakening people to their need for the spiritual and the communal, their needs for God and community. Another person explained: Marketing is transforming the negative or passive energies of disinterest, boredom, or even disdain into curiosity, interest, felt need, and taking action, or buying the product. In the case of evangelization, the product could be imagined as a relationship with Christ and the church.

Over the years, this explanation of evangelization has stayed with me. In fact, I have learned a powerful lesson both from Tom Peters and others in leadership positions in the business community. Effective business leaders have a passion for their products and a growing awareness of how to influence people. Rather than dismissing business people as simply being an expression of the secular world, church people need to learn from their passion and their techniques. As the church lumbers along, as the last hierarchy to admit its inefficiency, or the last expression of totalitarian governance to go unchallenged, the words of Jesus in Matthew 21:43 come to mind: "I tell you, the Kingdom of God will be taken away from you and given to those who will yield a rich harvest." Often I wonder if the success of twelve-step recovery processes and evangelical churches that employ well some of the techniques of the business world are not evidence that the torch of the mission of God's Reign is indeed being passed from the confines of organizational religion to other groups—with passion and missiological techniques.

Indeed, evangelization is at least in part marketing in a pure, altruistic sense. We have a treasure that we ought to want to share with others—faith-spirituality, and the Body of Christ, the Christian community. Especially as we look toward younger generations, generation "X" as it is called today (those in their twenties), and baby boomers in their thirties and forties and their children, we need as a church to embrace a greater spirit of innovation about mission. Many young adults in America, as a result of recent scandals in the church, poor catechesis while growing up, or stereotypic thinking about organized, mainline churches, have an aversion to the Roman Catholic Church and mainline Protestantism. Not in the name of attracting numbers, but rather because of a passion and conviction about what the church has to offer people, we need to fan passion and develop techniques for marketing/evangelizing.

The original title of the bishops' plan for evangelization was not *Go and Make Disciples* (a laudable title). It was instead *So Much to Give*. This earlier version bore down on the richness of the Catholic Christian tradition, indeed, how much the church has to offer contemporary society. The ear-

- Excellent weekend worship (good preaching, presiding, and proclamation, hospitality, congregational-style music)

- Ministries of religious education, worship, pastoral care, youth, finances, and administration, all well coordinated in boards, teams, or core communities that implement a holistic plan for each subdivision; utilizing the twelve steps for systems highlighted in this book.

- A parish leadership community that is comprised of discerned leaders from each of the aforementioned ministry groups.

- Various other programs that address real life, often pre-evangelical/human needs of the community. These ministries/programs are often of the healing nature or target needs specific to certain age demographic groups (twenties, thirties, midlife, seniors).

- Organizations that gather people around social life, entertainment, etc.

- These status quo efforts need to be joined to an innovative ministry—that of neighborhood minister, parish representative in a neighborhood, parish messenger (or other titles).

The role of this minister is to:
- visit ten to fifteen homes at least quarterly
- drop off a parish newsletter that communicates recent or upcoming events in the parish
- engage in conversations about needs in the parish, how the parish can better serve the neighborhood
- connect with needy or or struggling people, especially the elderly, widowed, or those living in some situation of need
- serve as a connecting person between people in the grassroots and the ministries or services of the parish or neighborhood
- if so discerned and decided upon, engage in ecumenical visitation, serving as a Christian representative to all denominations.

- This is where most people will be met in parish life.

- These efforts need to be structured for efficiency, pastoral sensitivity, welcome long-term care of souls, love of people, and a passion for excellence.

- This ministry furthers parish contact with the disconnected, the needy, those who have not yet had a spiritual awakening.

- In addition to connecting people to needed services, this ministry also recruits for processes like the catechumenate, returning/reconciling with the church, small groups, parish-based retreats and other parish efforts.

DIAGRAM 5

lier version highlighted the reluctance Catholics have to share, invite, evangelize—do marketing. There are many values the tradition of the church offers people. As I discussed evangelization recently with a group of parishioners in Woodland Hills, California (St. Mel's parish), three points emerged on both the hungers people have and food the church has to satisfy those hungers.

- Contemporary people in special, heartfelt ways crave meaning.

- So many individuals and families also hunger and thirst for interior healing.

- Though often not reflected upon, contemporary people hunger and thirst for human connection—that is, relationships and community.

If, through the grace of God, parishes could "spread the word" that they are oases for meaning, healing, and connection—rather than reservoirs of traditionalistic structures, obligations, ordinances, and rituals—we would begin to touch more lives. I also personally believe that the centerpiece of a new evangelization, or a new spirit of marketing, needs to be a synergistic contagion among church members, wherein through informal contacts with the unchurched or the disconnected, those not currently involved in community life are invited to become involved. A pioneer in the evangelization-catechetical movement, Johannes Hofinger, said many years ago that it is the community itself, passionately invested in Word, worship, and service, that becomes a kind of magnetic force attracting people to itself.

Let us return to the microworld, the local organism of the parish. As I said in the chapter on pastoral planning, it may be the role of centralized authority (i.e., the diocese or pasto-

STATUS QUO OF PARISH LIFE

(1) Weekend worship—at worship parishioners are encouraged to invite those they know in need of Christ and church to worship and parish activities

(2) Ministries

(3) Parish governance

(4) Programs addressing needs

(5) Organizations

(6) Neighborhood ministry representatives

(2)(3)(4)(5) gradually taking on communally the aspects of prayer and Scripture-sharing, life-sharing, joined to ministry

THE COMMUNAL PARISH

(1) Small faith groups becoming communities

(2) Processes of reentry for nominal members

(3) Households choosing household-based pilots for religious education

(4) Families and individuals in initiation-based pilots of catechesis and sacramental preparation

(5) Awakened Catholic Christians in various tracks of school of ministry

(6) Five percent of parish budget to marketing the parish

DIAGRAM 6

ral center) to serve as an advocate for heart-values, but the only effective way to proceed in terms of evangelization planning is on the level of small units, the parish, clusters of parishes, or deaneries. Let us try to imagine a marketing plan for a parish or a cluster that integrates some of the highlights of this book.

It seems to me that a first step on the part of the staff and parish council leadership is to re-imagine the status quo of parish life, not in a posture of maintenance, but rather as an integral piece of a larger, wholistic plan for evangelizing. Thus, the status quo of much of parish life may reflect the volunteer ministries, programs, and organizations of the postconciliar parish, but they are no longer goals unto themselves, but rather entry-level pieces in a larger mission-oriented, marketing plan (see Diagram 5, pp. 150–51).

Our marketing plan for parish life assumes the wedge or funnel metaphor that we explained before. We cannot be so naive as to think that everyone is ready or willing to engage in the behaviors of a small Christian community. The parish ought to be, nonetheless, poised to be intentionally moving in a direction (see Diagram 6, p. 153).

There is a reality in planning called "the page you never show," and perhaps that is what we have been discussing so far in this chapter. The ordinary parishioner coming to church perhaps does not need to know up front all the deliberation that had led up to the marketing plan, or the missiological strategy just articulated. In fact, for many it would be too much to assimilate. But those in church leadership need to break out of completely reactive approaches to ministry and to develop proactive marketing plans that have a broad-based people coverage and teleological—purposeful—intentionality. Those in leadership are responsible for touching as many lives as possible with an invitation to God's communal Reign.

12

Generation "X" and Midlifers

*W*hile I believe the entire content of this book contains important ideas for positioning the church more and better for mission work, I feel these strategies are inadequate against some powerful cultural realities. One is the whole secularized, anti-institutional religion, but spiritually seeking lifestyle of young baby boomers in their early to mid-thirties, and those born in the late sixties and early seventies, the latter being referred to as generation "X." As I listen to these people in one-on-one and group encounters, they portray a real spiritual movement in their lives, a kind of breaking apart of some of the pieces of their lives, that is prompting genuine spiritual seeking. Dr. Gilbert Bilezekian of Wheaton College has said for some time, as I reported in *Parishes That Excel,* that churches wanting to evangelize late baby boomers and generation "X" need to employ all the strategies in this book and more. Motivated churches need to evangelize, do mission work through the lens of youth and young adult culture. Bilezekian and his disciples, as well as others in the megachurch movement, are speaking the truth when they remind us that traditional, hierarchical rituals will not speak to the people of the video generation. Many innovative movements and also movements within mainline churches are trying a synthesis of music, drama, preaching, positive theology, and often alternative places to church to engage this age group.

I was reminded of this challenge and opportunity recently when I was in the Archdiocese of Los Angeles consulting with two parishes, St. Mel's in Woodland Hills and Holy Cross in Moorpark. I came across some information on a nearby effort at a Simi Valley Presbyterian church, a weekly event called "Sunday Evening Live." This Presbyterian church continues to offer its rather contemporary services at 8:00 A.M. and 9:30 A.M. on Sundays with a more traditional offering with organ music at 11:00 A.M. But at 6:00 P.M. on Sunday nights, a different kind of service is offered at the Simi Valley–Moorpark Association of Realtors Hall. Pastor Jeff Cheadle explains the innovation as "getting out of the church to get into the community." The "Sunday Night Live" celebration is an outreach to people who do not feel comfortable attending traditional church services or people who feel called more to a celebration with their families, or workers who cannot make daytime services. The service is described as an upbeat combination of message and music, the latter provided by a live rock band. The theology presented in the preached message is the positive theology of God's love— *really* good news, as Cheadle would put it. The service seeks to be enjoyable and informal, leaving participants with a good, positive feeling to take with them into the rest of the week.

These are evenings that appeal to adults, teens, and children together in one group. The event offers child care for infants and toddlers who might become a little squirmy during the service. To promote the beginning of this ministry, the Presbyterian church sent out professionally done, full-color flyers to the homes in the area. Cheadle describes

"Sunday Night Live" as an established church trying to do things in a fresh, exciting way. Sponsored by a church, it is deliberately not churchy. The services are open to the public. It is hoped that they will attract spiritual seekers who gradually may become part of a community of faith. A visionary board within the church has pledged money, resources, and personnel to make this ministry a reality.

In a similar move, Sunrise Christian Fellowship in Simi Valley uses alternative church music at its services. The musical groups include in their repertories Christian rock, country music, and jazz. The leadership at Sunrise believes music ministry is an important part of church life. Church music, they contend, ought both to give a message and be entertaining. Music creates an ambiance or environment in the church, and is certainly an integral part of imparting the message. Similarly, in nearby Moorpark, the Shiloh Community Church has for leadership in its music ministry the "Not Your Average Church Music" band. Frances Hales, director of its music ministry, explained recently, "We were children of the 1960s and 1970s. We decided not to go traditional with our worship music from the very beginning." Hales's combination of country rock, rock and roll, and Latin jazz attracts large numbers of young families. Recently Shiloh has moved from the old church building it gathered in to an abandoned warehouse, where a congregation member, a sound engineer, designed a state-of-the-art sound system for the old building.

Researching these three California churches reminded me of the work of megachurch movements that appeared in *Parishes That Excel*. Since the writing of that book, I have been more and more struck by the sociological data coming our way regarding the children of the 1960s and 1970s. Richard Schoennher, in *Full Pews, Empty Altars*, reports a real gutting of the male, celibate priesthood as a species that just is not reproducing itself in these age groups. Wade Clark Roof in *A Generation of Seekers* depicts the people populating the baby boomer generation and their offspring (in some cases, Generation "X") as people awakening to the spiritual and meaning dimensions of life, but not feeling compelled to go to their churches of origin for nurturance, but rather to places and congregations that feed them through the lens of the culture with which they are familiar. To put it another way, obvious, traditional church culture is a culture with which they are indeed unfamiliar and uncomfortable. The 1993 Gallup study on young Catholics was quite revealing. In the period from 1987 to 1993:

- the number of young Catholics saying that they could be good Catholics and disagree with the church's teaching on abortion increased by 17 percent;

- the number saying that the laity ought to have input into the use of parish income increased by 17 percent;

- the number comfortable with lay administrators of parishes and nonresidential priests rose by 17 percent.

The number claiming that they could be good Catholics and

- not be part of the church community: 73 percent of the study;

- disagree with the church's teaching on birth control: 73 percent of the study;

- disagree with the church's stand on divorce and remarriage: 62 percent of the study;

- not believe in the infallibility of the pope: 50 percent of the study;

- not be married in the Catholic Church: 61 percent of the study;

- not be concerned about or involved with the poor: 52 percent of the study;

- not offer stewardship or financial treasure to a faith community: 57 percent of the study;

- be in favor of a married priesthood: 72 percent of the study;

- be in favor of the ordination of women: 79 percent of the study.

The Gallup organization points to a healthy ecumenism among younger Catholics, but a very fluid sense of Catholic identity. From the study, it is hard to discern what young Catholics believe to be Catholic identity. In many of the talks I have given recently, I have been suggesting that, in the face of diffuse Catholic identity, perhaps it is time for those in pastoral leadership to articulate the heart-values of our church. Rather than values that derive mostly from the institution, perhaps a renewed sense of heart-values might include the Catholic Church being the church:

- committed to pursue what Jesus meant when he preached and revealed the Reign of God;

- that is a safe harbor for younger adults;

- that is a safe harbor for recent immigrants;

- that is staunchly committed to the values of social justice, to the point of serious self-scrutiny regarding intramural injustice within the church;

- committed to a sacramental way of life that is sensitive to God's self-manifestation in everyday experience, not just in pursuit of seven holy objects or rituals;

- committed to mending the clan, or the family;

- committed to the communal life, especially parishes consisting of small groups;

- known for its sharing of *meaning, healing, and connection*.

If the church is to evangelize, welcome baby boomers and generation "X," I think we need to employ all of the skills spoken of earlier in evangelization—pastoral planning and in creating a marketing strategy. I think we need to add, however, alternative forms of worship besides the Eucharist. While the Eucharist should remain the bedrock of prayer-worship, we must realize that many young people are not ready for or appreciative of the Eucharist. I think we are desperately in need of the kind of worship services just described at Sunrise, Shiloh, or the Simi Valley Presbyterian church's "Sunday Night Live." When folks and friends have been spiritually strengthened through such services, they then could be invited to more profound experiences of worship via the Eucharist, and more profound experiences of group life and family religious education/sacramental preparation. So as Diagram 7 indicates, we would need to add to our previous marketing strategy:

The leadership for such liturgical expansion cannot come from the current group of parish priests, nor from those recently coming out of seminary experiences. Catholic seminaries are simply not preparing clergy for mission, and those of us committed to evangelization who are priests are either too old or not equipped for the kind of culturally sensitive worship I believe younger people are in need of.

STATUS QUO OF PARISH LIFE	THE COMMUNAL PARISH
Excellent worship, with parishioners being encouraged, revisioned to invite those they know in need of Christ and the church to worship and parish activities —Excellent celebration of Eucharist —Excellent alternative worship services consisting of drama, contemporary music, and preaching	Parish life increasingly experienced in small groups and communities

DIAGRAM 7

I feel the same is true relative to the drain-off or bleeding away of Hispanics, Asians, and other recent immigrants to the United States to evangelical groups. While I documented the excellent work that Father Richard Broach and St. Michael's parish in Milwaukee are doing in mixing cultures in the multicultural ministry in the parish (see *Parishes That Excel*), I also believe that, in a spirit of inculturation, parishes and parishes within parishes need to be established that are the equivalent of our old national parishes. While a priest-figure may be important in such culturally sensitive experiments or pilots, the real leadership will need to come from the laity.

In terms of both young adults and ethnic subgroups, Catholic leadership needs to eat some humble pie and learn from the evangelical movements. While we need not espouse fundamentalist theology or take a literal approach to Scripture, we need to *benchmark* these churches on the reach-out to the young and racial-ethnic groups. We need to replicate some of what they do in our own pilots and model innovations. To fail to accept this challenge with immediacy is going to push the Catholic Church more and more toward the European Catholic experience of the church being the church of the old, or senior citizens, certainly not vital or relevant to the people or issues of today.

I mentioned earlier the midlife age group (my own age-group), aging baby boomers moving through midlife to senior years. It has been my experience that midlife is a deeply spiritual time, with lots of reevaluation going on of previous life structures and vocational decisions. Recently I have told friends that I believe midlife is the journey from the false ego to spirit, soul, or self. In the midst of this frequently lonely journey, midlifers are often burdened not only with their own family responsibilities but are also taking care of parents and others from the family of origin. Job loss, parenting one's adolescents and one's own parents, shifts in marriage and marital systems, grieving, depression, stress, and passing the halfway mark of life expectancy are tremendous issues for which folks need direction and mentoring.

For the young adult, the recent immigrant, the midlifers becoming seniors, empty ritual no longer suffices. Creative, communal-based ministries need to become part of the pastoral planning, evangelization planning, and marketing strategy if we want to prevent huge numbers of people from "going elsewhere" for faith nurturance, or going nowhere in frustration and disappointment.

Remember the Movement for a Better World's assessment that 75 percent of the potential congregation in every parish no longer walks with the Catholic community out of alienation or lack of interest. Could it be that our "full pews" really are not as full as they seem, that Catholic parishes are intoxicated with the superficial appearance of things?

Without some creative intervention, I fear someone's next study might be called *Empty Pews, Empty Altars*.

Epilogue

*E*arlier in the book, I spoke of the work of Paul VI, John Paul II, and many other ecclesial pronouncements— all at least notionally advancing the cause of evangelization.

What strikes me after years of work in evangelization is the gap I perceive between our spoken ideals and actual praxis on the level of pastoral ministry. If evangelization could happen through good will we would be doing quite well, for the church is full of good will. But we are "stuck" on the level of structure. In *Parishes That Excel*, I wrote about the need for flexible and adaptable structures that fit the mission of the Kingdom of God. Pastoral ministers need to be encouraged by church leaders to value and practice the re-imagining of parish life and innovation in the praxis of parish life. Instead, as Gerald Arbuckle tells us, we find ourselves in a period of restorationism, in which pre-Vatican II attitudes and styles of parish abound and are multiplying. Innovators, people with re-imagining abilities are silenced, ignored, or themselves go into exile out of frustration.

What is true in any form of individual, couple, or family therapy is also true in church life: things do not get better by waiting for someone else to change or do something. Growth occurs when individuals claim ownership and responsibility and redirect their own lives. In a sense, the church can change in a nanosecond if more and more of us decide that our parishes cannot and will not be held hostage by mediocrity and poor leadership. These nanosecond-type decisions need to be followed up with responsible, imaginative, innovative, entrepreneurial strategies, designed in a spirit of collaboration, community, and love—of God, one another, and the ever-evolving mystery of the church of Jesus Christ.

Bibliography

CHAPTER ONE

Johnson, Elizabeth. *Consider Jesus*. New York: The Crossroad Publishing Company, 1992.

McBrien, Richard P. *Catholicism, Volumes I and II*. Minneapolis: Winston Press, 1980.

Pope Paul VI. *Evangelii Nuntiandi*. Washington, DC: United States Catholic Conference, 1975.

Quastan, Johannes. *Patrology*. Utrecht-Antwerp: Spectrum Publishers, 1966.

Senior, Donald, C.P., and Carroll Stuhlmueller, O. P. *The Biblical Foundations for Mission*. Maryknoll, NY: Orbis, 1983.

Tillich, Paul. *Systematic Theology, Volumes I, II and III*. Chicago: The University of Chicago Press, 1967.

CHAPTER TWO

Braxton, Edward K. *The Wisdom Community*. New York: Paulist Press, 1980.

DiGiacomo, James, and John Walsh. *Encounter Series*. Minneapolis: Winston Press, 1978.

Holmes, Urban T. *Turning to Christ*. New York: Seabury Press, 1981.

Wallas, Jim. *The Call to Conversion*. San Francisco: Harper & Row, 1981.

CHAPTER THREE

Arbuckle, Gerald, A., S.M. *Refounding the Church*. New York: Orbis Books, 1993.

Covey, Steven. *The Seven Habits of Highly Effective People*. New York: Simon & Schuster, 1991.

Hoge, Dean R. *Future of Catholic Leadership*. Kansas City: Sheed & Ward, 1987.

Schwartz, Robert M. *Servant Leaders of the People of God*. New York: Paulist Press, 1989.

CHAPTER FOUR

Champlin, Joseph M. *The Visionary Leader*. New York: The Crossroad Publishing Company, 1993.

Morris, Thomas, *RCIA: Transforming the Church*. Mahwah, NJ: Paulist Press, 1989.

O'Meara, Thomas Franklin, O.P. *Theology of Ministry*. Ramsey, NJ: Paulist Press, 1983.

Osborne, Kenan B., O.F.M. *Ministry*. New York: Paulist Press, 1993.

CHAPTER FIVE

Kleissler, Thomas A., Margo A. LeBert, Mary C. McGuinness. *Small Christian Communities*. New York: Paulist Press, 1991.

Peck, M. Scott, M.D. *A World Waiting to Be Born*. New York: Bantam Books, 1993.

Schaef, Anne Wilson. *Beyond Therapy, Beyond Science*. San Francisco: HarperCollins Publishers, 1992.

Wuthnow, Robert. *Sharing the Journey*. New York: Macmillan, 1994.

CHAPTER SIX

Groome, Thomas H. *Sharing Faith*. New York: HarperCollins Publishers, 1991.

Guzie, Tad. *The Book of Sacramental Basics*. Ramsey, NJ: Paulist Press, 1981.

CHAPTER SEVEN

Callahan, Kennon, *Effective Church Leadership: 12 Keys to An Effective Church*. San Francisco: Harper & Row, 1990.
Cappellaro, Juan Bautista. *From A Crowd to the People of God*. Rome: Better World Movement, 1983.
Schaller, Lyle E. *Growing Plans*. Nashville: Abingdon Press, 1983.

CHAPTER EIGHT

The Gallup Organization. *The Unchurched American*. Princeton, NJ: Gallup Organization, 1988.
Harmony, Sarah. *Re-Membering Church*. Collegeville, MN: The Liturgical Press, 1991.
National Conference of Catholic Bishops. *Go and Make Disciples: Shaping a Catholic Evangelizing People*. Washington, D.C.: United States Catholic Conference, 1993.
Savage, John. *The Apathetic and Bored Church Member*. Pittsford: L.E.A.D. Consultants, 1976.

CHAPTER NINE

Haring, Bernard. *Evangelization Today*. New York: The Crossroad Publishing Company, 1991.

CHAPTER TEN

Brennan, Patrick. *F.L.A.M.E.: Full Cycle Youth Evangelization*. Allen, TX: Tabor, 1993.
Senge, Peter M. *The Fifth Discipline*. New York: Doubleday, 1900.

CHAPTER ELEVEN

Peters, Thomas. *Thriving on Chaos*. New York: Alfred A. Knopf, 1987.

CHAPTER TWELVE

The Gallup Organization. *U.S. Catholicism Trends in the 90s*. Princeton: Gallup Organization, 1993.

Roof, Wade Clark. *A Generation of Seekers: Spiritual Journeys*. San Francisco: Harper & Row, 1993.

Shoennher, Richard. *Full Pews, Empty Altars*. Madison, WI: University of Wisconsin Press, 1993.